The ABC *of Cookery*

IMPERIAL WAR MUSEUM

First published by the Ministry of Food in 1945

First published in this format in 2008 by
Imperial War Museum
Lambeth Road, London SE1 6HZ
www.iwm.org.uk

Please note the information in this book was issued by the
Ministry of Food in 1945 and must not be taken as
Government or Imperial War Museum advice

ISBN 978-1-904897-99-6

Printed by Graphicom, Italy

The ABC of Cookery

This is not a recipe book. It is a book which explains cookery *methods*: methods useful in days of plenty as well as in times of rationing. It tells, for instance, how to boil, bake and fry; how to make pastry and, having made it, how to line a basin or top a pie with it. The indignant bride who wrote complaining that cake recipes always ended with the words: "mix to the usual cake consistency" and how could she be expected to know what that was, will find her problem solved on page 73. In short, this book tells how to carry out all the different cookery processes and explains what cookery terms mean. It is intended to be used with the Ministry of Food Recipe Leaflets, although it is not restricted to war-time cookery.

But one thing the war years have taught us is that good cooking, important in itself, is not enough. The housewife must know how to plan her family's meals. Her choice of food will largely determine not only their good health but also their good looks! Proper feeding can go a long way towards ensuring clear eyes, glossy hair, skin that is free from blemishes, just as your resistance to infection is largely determined by the food you eat. For this reason a chapter on "How to Plan Meals" has been included. It is well worth the closest study.

Mininstry of Food, 1945.

Contents

Page

1. **THE CHOICE AND CARE OF COOKING UTENSILS**. — including list of cooking equipment for two people. 1

2. **SHOPPING TIPS**. — Quantities of perishable food to buy for two people 6
STORING FOOD. — Choice of cupboard — Perishable foods — Vegetables — Fruit — Food Containers — Care of Stores. 8

3. **COOKING TERMS AND METHODS**. — Au gratin — Baking — Basting — Batters — Beating — Blanching — Blending — Boiling — Bouquet garni — Braising — Breadcrumbs — Brush with egg and milk — Caramelise — Casserole — Cereals — Coat — Consistency — Cream the fat — Croutons — Cut and fold — Dice — Dissolve — Dot — Dough — Dredge — Dripping — Dry ingredients — Fat — Fillet — Forcemeat — Frying — Garnish — Gelatine — Glaze — Grate — Grilling — Knead — Marinade — Mixing — Parboiling — Poaching — Pulses — Purée — Raising agents — Raspings — Roux — Scald — Sear — Seasoned flour — Sift — Simmering — Skewer — Sousing — Steaming — Steep — Stewing — Stock — Temperature — Tepid — Whip — Zest. 9

4. **USING RECIPES**. — How to weigh and measure — Table of weights and handy measures. 17

5. **HOW TO SEASON FOOD**. — Bay leaves — Capers — Cayenne pepper — Celery seed — Chillies — Chives — Cinnamon — Cloves — Curry powder — Essences — Garlic — Ginger — Horseradish — Lemons — Mace — Marjoram — Mint — Mustard — Nutmeg — Onions — Orange — Paprika — Parsley — Pepper — Sage — Salt — Sugar — Thyme — Vinegar. 19

6. **MILK AND CHEESE**. — Fresh milk — To scald milk — Keeping milk fresh — Dried milk — Evaporated milk — Condensed milk — Sour milk — Some ways of using milk in the menu — Cooking cheese — Making cheese sauce — Some ways of using grated cheese. 22

7. **EGGS**. — Storing eggs — The effect of heat on eggs — How to prepare shell eggs for cooking — How to prepare dried eggs for cooking — Dried eggs used dry — How to beat eggs — How to boil shell eggs — Coddled eggs — How to hard boil dried eggs — How to poach shell eggs — How to scramble eggs — How to make an omelette — How to make custards with shell or dried eggs. 24

8. **FISH**. — Kinds of fish and best methods of serving — Buying fresh fish — How to prepare fish for cooking — How to boil fish — How to steam fish — How to grill fish — How to fry fish — How to bake fish — How to stew fish — Using up cooked or canned fish — How to carve whole fish — What to serve with fish. 29

9. **MEAT, GAME AND POULTRY**. — What good meat looks like — Why meat is cooked — Cuts of meat and their uses — How to prepare meat for cooking — How to prepare poultry for cooking — How to prepare hares and rabbits for cooking — How to boil unsalted or fresh meat, game and poultry 34

— How to boil salted meat — How to stew — Roasting — Pot roasting — Braising — How to fry meat — How to grill meat — Carving — What to serve with meat, game and poultry.

10. **VEGETABLES AND SALADS**. — Storing vegetables — Ways of cooking and serving vegetables — How to boil green and root vegetables — How to cook vegetables in fat — How to boil dried peas, beans and lentils — How to boil potatoes — Steaming vegetables — How to fry vegetables — How to bake vegetables — Suitable vegetables for salads — Tips for the salad maker — Salad dressings. 49

11. **FRUIT**. — How to prepare fruit — How to serve fruit raw — Fresh fruit salad — How to stew fresh fruit — How to stew dried fruit — Stewing fruit in the oven — How to bake apples and pears — How to make a fruit purée or pulp — How to make fruit pies, puddings, etc. 54

12. **FATS, OILS and FRYING**. — Storage — Fats suitable for pastry, cakes and puddings — Fats suitable for frying — How to render fat — How to clarify fat — How to prepare suet for pastry — How to prepare food for frying — Shallow or dry frying — Deep-fat frying. 58

13. **STOCK, SOUPS AND SAUCES**. — Bone stock — Vegetable stock — Emergency stock — Fish stock — Keeping stock — How to make a mixed vegetable soup — How to make a cream soup — Thickenings used for sauces — Proportions for thickening — How to make a sauce — How to make thick gravy. 63

14. **BEVERAGES**. — How to make tea — How to make coffee — How to make cocoa. 66

15. **CEREALS, CEREAL PRODUCTS AND STARCH**. — Storing cereals — Cooking cereals and starches — How to make a mould with rice, oatmeal, semolina or sago — How to make a mould with cornflour or arrowroot — How to make baked milk puddings using rice, tapioca, sago and barley — How to boil rice — How to boil macaroni, spaghetti, etc. — How to make oatmeal porridge. 69

16. **SUGAR**. — Storing sugar and jam — The effect of heat on sugar — Temperatures used in sweet making. 72

17. **BATTERS, CAKES AND PASTRY**. — Doughs — Cake and pudding mixtures — Batters — What makes batters, cakes and doughs light? — Proportions of raising agent to use with National flour — The kinds of flour used in baking — Tips in mixing batters — Sponges — Creamed mixtures — Rubbed-in mixtures — What should a good cake look like? — Common faults in cake making and their causes — Steamed puddings — Boiled puddings — Soft doughs — How to make scones — What makes pastry tough and hard? — How to make short pastry — How to make rough flaky pastry — How to make hot water pastry or "raised" pies — How to make suet pastry — How to make a flan — How to make a double crust tart — How to make an open tart — How to make a lattice top — How to cover a pie — How to line a basin with pastry — Biscuits — Baking time-table. 73

18. BREAD AND SANDWICHES. — How to keep the loaf fresh — To avoid dry loaf ends — Preparation of breadcrumbs — Making toast — Uses for stale bread — Tips in making sandwiches. 87

19. HOW TO PLAN MEALS. — Three rules for fitness — Pattern of meals that follow the rules for healthy eating — Breakfast menu — Mid-morning snack — Dinner menu — Tea menu — Supper or lunch menu — Rules for good meal planning — Packed meals — Preparing meals. 88

N.B. — weight and temperature conversion charts can be found on pages 95–96.

1 *The Choice and Care of Cooking Utensils*

It is just as important to have the right tools of good quality for cooking as for any other highly skilled job. One does not find a carpenter, tool-maker or any other craftsman content to use cheap and shoddy tools. They know it is impossible to obtain first-class results with poor equipment.

Beginners are advised to choose a few very good utensils and to add to them gradually as they are able. Make sure of having at least the following utensils of first-class quality: saucepans, frying pan, kitchen scales, a vegetable knife and a cook's knife, a potato peeler, baking trays and cake tins, and a half-pint or pint measuring jug.

Saucepans

Whether aluminium, iron, enamel or steel, saucepans should be of a good thick quality. This is important with all kinds of stoves. Thin pans are bad because they cook unevenly and make the food stick and burn.

All saucepans should have well-fitting lids and, preferably, lids which are smooth and free from unnecessary grooves and ridges which make cleaning difficult.

Frying Pans

It is very important to have a heavy frying pan the bottom of which will remain flat. Thin pans soon buckle with the result that the food cooks unevenly, burning in some spots and not cooking in others.

Kitchen Scales

The scales which have separate weights are more accurate and last longer than the spring-balance type (see page 18).

Kitchen Knives

It is very difficult to do good kitchen work with table knives. Try to have one good cook's knife and one vegetable knife and keep them sharp.

A good potato peeler will be found a great help.

Cake Tins, Roasting Pans and Baking Trays

These should be of a heavy quality which will remain flat with use. Thin pans bend with the heat of the oven and cakes cooked in them will rise and brown unevenly. Baking trays with the edge turned up all round are the most practical as the edge prevents liquid and grease from falling into the oven. These are sometimes provided with the stove.

Pie Dishes and Casseroles

Casseroles are baking dishes or pie dishes with lids and in some cases the lids themselves are deep enough to use for baking. These dishes are economical when equipment must be limited. Saucepans with short handles may also be used as casseroles. Casseroles and pie dishes may be made of china or glass (both fireproof), enamelware, aluminium or steel.

The following table gives the utensils desirable for a well-equipped kitchen for two people. There are also suggestions for improvising if it is not possible to have all this equipment at first.

Item	*Size*	*Number*
Saucepan with lid	1½ pints	2
Ditto	3 pints	1
Ditto	8 pints	1
All of good heavy quality. If some have short handles they may do duty as casseroles.		
Frying pan	8" diameter	1
Very thick heavy quality iron, steel or aluminium.		
Kettle	3 pints	1
Good quality.		
Double boiler	3 pints	1
Quality as for saucepans. If not available a basin on top of a saucepan will serve the same purpose.		
Steamer	8" diameter	1
Quality as for saucepans. This should be bought to fit in the 8-pint saucepan.		
Cake tin	6" diameter	1
Sandwich tins	6" diameter	2
Bun tins	Set of 1 doz.	1
Roasting pan	Size to fit oven with 2" clearance between pan and oven walls	1
Heavy quality which will not buckle with the heat of the oven.		
Baking trays	Ditto	2
Heavy iron or steel.		
Enamel or other deep plate	8" diameter	1

Item	*Size*	*Number*
Kitchen scales	–	1
Government stamped and with separate weights ¼ oz. to 7 lb.		
Pie dish	1½ pints	1
Ditto	3 pints	1
Casserole with lid	1½ pints	1
Or have two casseroles 1½ pint and 3 pint, with deep lids suitable for use as baking dishes. Saucepans with short handles may be used instead of casseroles.		
Pudding basin	6" diameter	1
Ditto	8" diameter	1
With straight sides.		
Mixing bowl	10" – 12" diameter	1
With rounded sides.		
Sieve	8" diameter	1
Gravy strainer	6" diameter	1
Collander	10" diameter	1
Flour sifter	–	1
It is a great asset to have all of these, but the 8" sieve could be made to do duty for the others.		
Flour dredger	–	1
Not essential as flour may be sprinkled by hand.		
Teaspoon, tablespoon, dessertspoon		1 of each size
Wooden spoons	10" long	2
Cook's spoon or ladle	–	1
Cook's spoon, perforated	–	1
Cook's knife	8" long	1
Vegetable knife	–	1
Stainless when available.		
Potato peeler	–	1
Vegetable knife will do, but is not as quick or economical.		
Palette knife	8" long	1
Stainless when available.		
Knife sharpener	–	1
Cook's fork	10" long	1
Stainless when available.		
Kitchen scissors	–	1
Fish slice	–	1
A perforated spoon will do instead.		
Egg whisk	8" long	1
A wire whisk is the most useful.		
Grater	–	1
Can opener	–	1
Corkscrew	–	1

Item	*Size*	*Number*
Salt and pepper containers	–	1 of each
A glass storage jar is the best for storing cooking salt. A pepper mill for home grinding of peppercorns gives the best flavoured pepper.		
Measuring jug	½ to 1 pint	1
Marked in ¼, ½ and ¾ pints.		
Scrubbing brush	4" long	1
For vegetables.		
Saucepan brush	–	1
Swabs	–	2
Oven cloths	–	2
Tea towels	–	6
Rolling pin	12" long	1
Preferably with loose handles. It is easier to roll lightly with these.		
Pastry board	20" by 12"	1
Not necessary if the table top is suitable.		
Chopping board	8" by 6"	1
Any small, thick piece of wood with a smooth surface will do.		
Potato masher	–	1
A cook's fork may be used, but is slow.		
Cake rack	12" by 8"	1
Wire.		
Pastry brush	–	1
Fingers may be used instead.		
Mincer	–	1
Chopping finely will do instead.		
Biscuit cutters	–	1 set
An empty tin may be used instead. The tin will cut more easily if a hole is pierced in the bottom.		
Sink tidy	–	1
Pie funnel	–	1
An egg cup may be used.		
Oven thermometer	–	1
Not necessary if the oven has a thermometer or heat regulator. See page 15.		
Sugar or fat thermometer	–	1
Not essential but useful for deep-fat frying, making sweets, making jam and fruit bottling. See pages 48 and 56.		
Refuse bin	–	1
With a lid.		
Storage bins	–	–
See page 8.		

The Care of Cooking Utensils

1. Keep them clean. Dirty cooking utensils not only spoil the flavour of food cooked in them but they also wear out more quickly.
2. Put all utensils to soak as soon as you have finished using them. Those which have been used for mixing cakes, flour mixtures, eggs or milk should be soaked in cold water. Hot water hardens these foods and makes them difficult to remove. Utensils used for cooking fish should also be soaked in cold water.
3. If food sticks or burns, soak the saucepans well before attempting to clean them. Avoid scratching the pan during cleaning. The same applies to cleaning pie dishes and casseroles.
4. Do not pour cold liquid into hot pans. This makes even the thickest pans buckle in time.
5. To obtain a smooth surface on frying pans for omelettes and pancakes rub well with a little cooking salt.

Aluminium Utensils

1. Washing soda and strong washing powders should not be used in the washing up water.
2. Always dry aluminium thoroughly after washing for if left wet the surface will soon become rough and pitted.
3. Steel wool is excellent for cleaning aluminium.

Enamel Utensils

1. If food sticks soak the pans well and avoid scouring which scratches the enamel. Boil salt water in a burnt pan and repeat the process until the burn is softened sufficiently to be easily removed.
2. Do not use chipped enamel as there is danger of small pieces of enamel coming off in the food. Poor quality enamel chips very easily.
3. Never put an empty pan on a hot stove or the enamel will soon crack and chip.

Tinned Utensils

These are generally tinned iron or tinned steel.

1. Try to prevent the tinning from being scratched by harsh scouring.
2. Always dry tinned utensils well after washing to prevent them from rusting. Dry with a cloth and finish off by standing in a warm place.
3. Baking trays and cake tins should be washed thoroughly but do not polish them. Food takes longer to brown in shiny tins.

N.B. — Zinc or galvanized iron utensils should not be used for cooking purposes. Copper utensils are satisfactory if the inside is frequently re-tinned and if they are kept scrupulously clean. Do not cook acid foods such as vinegar, lemons, etc., in copper.

Steel Utensils

1. Keep them clean and free from scratches.
2. Dry thoroughly after washing.
3. Any cutlery which is not stainless should be kept well polished.

Fireproof Glass, Earthenware and China Utensils

1. Soak clean and avoid unnecessary scouring.
2. Although these dishes stand up to great heat and cold, care should be taken not to ill treat them. For example, do not plunge a very hot dish straight into cold water.

Wooden Utensils

Keep them clean and well scoured. Dry thoroughly.

2 *Shopping Tips*

1. Shopping is very much easier if you have worked out your week's menu in advance, or at least two or three days in advance and know exactly what to buy. For menu planning see pages 92–93.
2. Learn about the food values of different groups of foods on pages 88–90. Then when one kind of food is unobtainable or too expensive you will be able to substitute a food of equal nutritive value.
3. Keep a pad or slate near the kitchen store cupboard and make a note when any supplies are running low. This list and your menu plan should help you to reduce the number of shopping trips to the minimum. It should not be necessary to buy non-perishable foods more than once a week.
4. Green vegetables and milk should be bought fresh every day. If you have a really cold larder, butter, fats, cheese and bacon need only be bought once a week. Meat will keep two or three days according to the kind of larder you have and the state of the meat when purchased. It is wise to buy fish, sausages and offal or meat sundries on the day you intend to cook them.
5. Do not buy more food at a time than can be used up while it is in first-class condition.
6. Foods in packages generally cost more than the same food sold loose.
7. Examine all purchases before storing away and if not in good condition return them to the shop at once.

8. For details of different cuts of meat, kinds of fish, etc., see appropriate section of this book.
9. Have an emergency shelf in your cupboard and keep it stocked with foods for preparing quick meals or for unexpected guests: for example, tinned or dried milk, dried eggs, canned or dried vegetables, bottled or canned fruits, canned meat and fish, meat or yeast extract for soups and stock, plain and sweet biscuits.

Quantities of Perishable Foods to Buy for Two People for One Meal

These quantities allow one average sized helping per person and must be adjusted to suit individual appetites. If catering for more than two, multiply the quantities accordingly.

Food	*Amount for Two*
FISH	
Whole fish	1½ lb.
Cutlets	1 lb.
Fillets	½–¾ lb.
MEAT	
Brains	1 pair, small
Breast and neck	1 lb.
Chops	2
Cutlets	2–4
Head, sheep's	1
Heart, lamb or ox or calf	1
Kidney, sheep's, pig's	3 or 4
Kidney, veal	2
Liver	6–8 oz.
Mince	½ lb.
Ox-tail	1
Cooked meats	4–6 oz.
Roasting meat	(3-lb. joint is the smallest which is really satisfactory.)
Sausages	½ lb.
Steak	½ lb.
Sweetbreads	1 pair
Tripe	½ lb.
Trotters	2
Calf's head	These all serve 6 or more people and are not suitable for buying in small amounts.
Ox tongue	
Pig's head	
FRUIT	
for cooking	1 lb.

Food	*Amount for Two*
VEGETABLES	
Artichokes, Jerusalem	1–2 lb.
Beans, French and runner	½–¾ lb.
Beetroot	1 lb.
Broad beans	1–2 lb.
Brussel Sprouts	½–1 lb.
Cabbage	½–¾ lb.
Carrots	½ lb.
Cauliflower	1 small
Celery	1 head
Kale	1 lb.
Lettuce	1 medium-sized
Parsnips	¾ lb.
Peas	1–1½ lb.
Potatoes	1 lb.
Spinach	1 lb.
Swede	1 lb.
Turnips	1 lb.
Watercress	¼ lb.

Storing Food

If possible choose food storing cupboards which are dry, well ventilated and light. The shelves should be within easy reach and it is better to have narrow shelves than deep ones. With deep shelves food may be pushed to the back and overlooked. Whenever possible the shelves should be painted. Dirt and dust can be easily wiped off painted surfaces whereas they stick to unpainted ones.

PERISHABLE FOODS, such as meat, milk, butter, bacon, etc., should be stored in a meat safe or cupboard by themselves. If this is not possible a separate shelf in the storage cupboard should be kept for such foods. A piece of muslin fastened at the edge of the shelf above the perishable food and hanging down over it is a very good idea to keep off dust and flies.

VEGETABLES should be stored on a well-ventilated rack or hung up in string bags. Ventilation is very important as if vegetables are kept without air and in the dark they may soon become mouldy. For salad vegetables see page 53.

FRUIT should be stored in the same way as vegetables or spread out on shallow dishes in a cool, airy place.

CONTAINERS. Glass jars with lids are the best for storing dry foods. It is easy to see what is in them and whether the food is keeping well. Glass does not affect the flavour of food. China jars are satisfactory if they have well-fitting lids. Tins are not as good, but if these are the only containers available they should be used in preference to keeping foods in paper bags. All containers should be labelled clearly.

Care of Stores

1. Clean out the store cupboard every week and inspect the condition of dry goods, including dried fruit, at frequent intervals, turning out the contents of each jar in turn. Constant inspection will prevent bugs or weevils from attacking the food. If bugs or weevils have got into the jars, wash the jars thoroughly. Dried fruit which has become infected should be washed and dried before use. Other food should be discarded.
2. See that all old supplies of any foods are finished up before new ones are started. Never put new supplies on top of old ones.
3. Mark the date of purchase on tinned foods and use them in the order in which they were purchased.

For further notes on the storage of foods see List of Contents.

3 *Cooking Terms and Methods*

AU GRATIN. This refers to a covering of browned breadcrumbs dotted with butter or margarine. It is used on top of a cooked dish of meat, fish, eggs or vegetables. The food may first be covered with a thick sauce. The gratin is then put under the grill or in a very hot oven to form a crisp brown crust. Serve in the dish in which it is cooked.

BAKING. This term is used to cover all foods which are cooked in an oven. Foods which are baked with a little fat are often spoken of as "roasted", for example, meat and potatoes. For suitable foods and methods of baking see the following sections:

Baking temperatures (pages 16 and 73).
Baking custards (page 28).
Baking fish (page 29–30).
Roasting meat, game and poultry (page 42).
Baking vegetables (page 52).
Baking fruit (page 57).
Baking milk puddings (page 70).
Batters, cake and pastry (page 73).

The important points to remember in baking are:

1. Do not waste oven space but fill the oven to capacity. This does not mean over-crowding. There must be room for hot air to circulate round all the dishes, or they will not cook evenly. Most ovens need to have a space of 2"–3" left between the oven walls and the dishes being cooked. Follow the advice of the makers of the stove.
2. Cook together foods which require the same temperatures, for example, a stew in a casserole with a rice pudding and some stewed fruit or a dish of soup or stock. For cooking temperatures see pages 16 and 73.

3. If baking foods which require different temperatures, for example, pastry, cakes and custard, start off with the foods which need the hottest oven and work down the temperature scale.
4. To obtain the best results it is important to place food correctly in the oven. Follow the advice of the maker in this as stoves vary a great deal and no general instruction can be given.

BASTING. This means keeping the surface of food moist by spooning liquid or melted fat over it during cooking (see "Roasting Meat", page 42, and "Grilling", page 13).

BATTERS. Mixtures of flour, egg, liquid and seasoning (see pages 73–74).

BEATING. This is a method of mixing air into such foods as batters, eggs, cream, etc. It is also used for making a mixture smooth and free from lumps, for example, a sauce. There are various kinds of hand and motor-driven beaters on the market, but a wooden spoon for thick mixtures and an egg whisk for thin mixtures are the most generally used. Beating is a vigorous motion and consists of turning the mixture over and over with a wide circular movement, to mix in as much air as possible (see also pages 26 and 76).

BLANCHING. **Method 1**. Dip food into boiling water for a few minutes, then plunge it into cold water. This is used for helping to remove the skins from tomatoes, peaches and almonds, or for shrinking fruit, for example apples, before packing it into preserving jars.

Method 2. Place the food in cold water and bring it to the boil. Remove the food and plunge it into cold water to cool it rapidly. This method is used for preparing offal or meat sundries for cooking (see pages 38–39).

BLENDING. This means mixing thoroughly. In the case of thickening a liquid with flour, blending is the term used to describe the process of mixing the flour to a smooth paste with a little cold liquid, before adding the hot liquid (see page 66).

BOILING. Strictly speaking this means cooking food in boiling water. (A liquid boils when the surface is continually agitated by large bubbles.) In practice, however, many "boiled" foods are cooked at a temperature below boiling point, that is, they are simmered or poached. All meats, fish, poultry and stews should be simmered. Vegetables, puddings, peas, beans, lentils, cereals, macaroni, spaghetti, etc., are boiled.

Sufficient heat should be applied to keep the liquid bubbling gently. Violent boiling should be avoided. It wastes fuel; it does not cook the food any faster; it tends to make the food break up and so spoils the appearance; the liquid is evaporated too quickly with the consequent danger of the food burning. There are one or two exceptions to this rule; for example, when one wants to drive off water quickly from syrup or a sauce to make it thicker, then violent boiling with the lid off hastens the process. For details of methods of boiling see the

following sections:
Boiling eggs (page 26).
Boiled custards (page 28).
Boiling fish (page 31).
Boiling meat (pages 40–41).
Boiling green and root vegetables (pages 49–50).
Boiling dried beans, lentils and split peas (page 51).
Boiling potatoes (page 51).
Boiling sauces (page 65).
Boiling beverages (page 66).
Boiling rice (page 71).
Boiling macaroni, spaghetti, etc. (page 71).
Boiling sugar (pages 72–73).

BOUQUET GARNI. A bunch of herbs used as flavouring for stocks, soups, stews and other savoury dishes. It consists of a small sprig of thyme, a small bay leaf (or a piece of one), and two sprigs of parsley tied together with thick thread. If fresh herbs are not available, tie the equivalent dried herbs in a piece of muslin. The bouquet garni must always be removed before the dish is served. It should be removed as soon as the food is sufficiently flavoured.

BRAISING. Means cooking food on a bed of vegetables in a covered pan or casserole. It is a combination of stewing and baking or pot roasting. Sufficient liquid is used to keep the food from burning and this liquid makes the gravy or sauce to serve with the dish. Meat is the food most commonly braised (see page 44), but vegetables, game and poultry are also cooked by this method.

BREAD CRUMBS. (See page 87.)

BRUSH WITH EGG OR MILK. This means to cover the surface of the food with an even coating of egg or milk. It is used for giving a shiny top to pastry, buns, etc., making the food brown more quickly and to a deeper shade. Special pastry brushes are made for this purpose (see page 4). Dried egg is more economical for brushing than fresh egg as only a small quantity need be mixed at a time (see also "Glaze").

CARAMELISE. To heat sugar until it turns brown (see page 72).

CASSEROLE. A baking dish with a tight-fitting lid, generally used for oven cooking of stews and similar dishes (see pages 1 and 2). The food is usually served from the casserole.

CEREALS. This includes all grains such as rice, wheat, oats, rolled oats and oatmeal, barley, semolina (see page 69).

COAT. To cover with a thin layer.

CONSISTENCY. The term used to describe the thickness or texture of a mixture, for example, batters and doughs (see page 73).

CREAM THE FAT. To beat softened fat with a wooden spoon until it is light and fluffy, the consistency of whipped cream (see page 76).

CROUTONS. Small pieces of toasted or fried bread used as an accompaniment to soup and sometimes for garnishing savoury dishes.

CUT AND FOLD. Is a method of mixing flour into a beaten mixture to avoid losing air already beaten in. The motion of the spoon is similar to that used in beating but the action is carried out very slowly and gently with the spoon being occasionally passed down through the middle of the mixture.

DICE. To cut in small cubes. The quickest way of doing this is to cut the food in long slices, cut the slices in strips and then, holding the bundle of strips together, cut across them to make small cubes. Use a chopping board to cut on. With vegetables such as onions, carrots, etc., do not make the cuts right to the end of the vegetable. The slices will hold together better this way.

DISSOLVE. To melt a solid food in a liquid. For example, sugar or salt will dissolve when mixed with water.

DOT. To put small pieces of food here and there on top of a dish. Generally fat is used.

DOUGH. A thick mixture of flour, liquid or other ingredient (see page 73).

DREDGE. To sprinkle lightly.

DRIPPING. Fat obtained from cooked meat or from pieces of fat rendered down (see page 59).

DRY INGREDIENTS. Ingredients such as flour, salt, sugar, baking powder, spices, etc.

FAT. Butter, margarine, suet, lard, cooking fat, bacon fat and dripping are all fats (see page 58).

FILLET. A piece of meat or fish without bone.

FORCEMEAT. A savoury stuffing.

FRYING. (See page 58, "Fats and Oils".)

GARNISH. Trimming or decoration.

GELATINE. Used for setting jellies. It is generally sold as granulated gelatine but may be sold in sheet form. Allow ½ oz.–¾ oz. per pint of liquid. Soak the gelatine for 10 minutes in a little cold liquid and then dissolve it in the remaining liquid which has been heated to boiling point. Add sweetening and flavouring. Packet jellies consist of gelatine, flavouring, colouring and sometimes sweetening. They should be prepared according to the directions on the packet.

GLAZE. This term is generally used for the process of brushing the tops of pies, buns, etc., with egg and water, sugar and water, or some preparation which improves the surface of the finished product. An egg glaze is generally brushed on before the food goes into the oven. A sugar and water glaze is put on when the food is cooked. A meat glaze consists of a clear stock, thickened by boiling to drive off most of the water.

GRATE. To shave into small shreds on a grater. Graters are divided into: coarse, used chiefly for vegetables, suet and sometimes cheese; fine, used for breadcrumbs, cheese, orange and lemon rind; very fine or nutmeg grater, used for nutmegs and for grating onion to extract the juice.

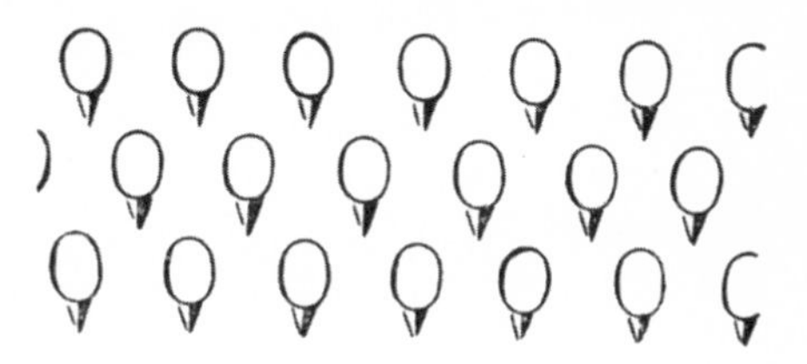

COARSE GRATER

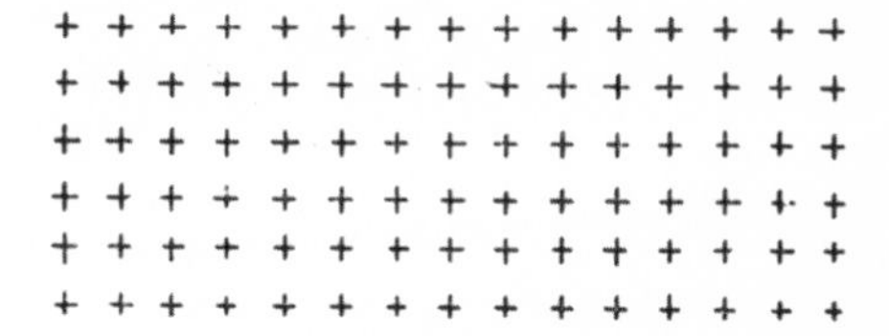

MEDIUM GRATER

FINE GRATER

GRILLING. This is cooking food by exposing it directly to a fierce red heat. Foods suitable for grilling are: beef steak (best cuts only); veal, mutton, lamb or pork chops; liver; bacon; kidneys; sausages; bacon; fish; tomatoes; apple rings; mushrooms; chicken; fish cakes; rissoles; hamburgers or meat balls. (Less fat is required to grill fish cakes and rissoles than to fry them.) The grill is also very useful for browning the tops of savoury dishes when the oven is not in use.

1. Follow the method of grilling recommended by the manufacturer of the stove but remember that the grill must be red-hot before cooking is started.
2. Grease the grill rack before placing the food on it.
3. Lean meat or rissoles and fish cakes need brushing with melted fat or oil before grilling and white fish needs basting (see page 10) with melted fat during cooking. Fatty fish such as herrings do not need brushing with fat. Small whole fish should have gashes cut in each side to allow the heat to penetrate to the centre.

4. Turn the food once or twice during grilling, taking care not to pierce the surface with a fork or the juices will run out. Foods which require more than 5 minutes' cooking (see table below) should be cooked more slowly after they have browned. The slower cooking is done either by reducing the heat of the grill or by moving the food further away from the heat. Over a coal or coke fire turn the food frequently.

GRILLING TIME-TABLE

Bacon	3–5 minutes, depending on the thickness.
Beef Steak	10–20 minutes, depending on the thickness and whether preferred underdone or well done.
Fish	5–20 minutes, depending on size and thickness.
Gammon Rasher	10–20 minutes, depending on size and thickness.
Kidneys	6–10 minutes
Liver	5–10 minutes, according to thickness.
Mushrooms	5–10 minutes
Mutton Cutlets	7–10 minutes
Mutton Chops	10–20 minutes
Pork or Veal Chops	20 minutes
Sausages	9–12 minutes

KNEAD. To work a dough lightly with the knuckles, by bringing the outside of the dough into the centre.

MARINADE. A mixture of vinegar, spices, herbs, etc., in which meat is steeped before cooking to improve the flavour and make it more tender. Oil is often added to the vinegar.

MIXING. Combining ingredients by stirring with a circular motion round the bowl or pan. This is a more gentle movement than beating and is not used for adding air to the mixture.

PARBOILING. This means partly boiling, generally for about half the normal time; cooking is then finished by some other method.

POACHING. (See "Simmering" below and "Eggs", page 24.)

PULSES. These are peas, beans, lentils and split peas (see page 49).

PURÉE. A fine pulp obtained by rubbing cooked fruit, vegetables or other food through a sieve.

RAISING AGENTS. Substances which produce a gas and make flour mixtures rise, e.g., yeast and baking powder (see page 75).

RASPINGS. Very fine crumbs obtained by grating the crust of stale bread on a fine grater. Browned breadcrumbs are sometimes called raspings (see page 87).

ROUX. A mixture of melted fat and flour cooked together. This is the first stage in making a sauce with fat (see page 65).

SCALD. (a) To heat a liquid to just under boiling point; or (b) to pour on boiling water. (To scald milk, see page 22.)

SEAR. To brown or form a coating on the surface of meat. A very high temperature is necessary to do this quickly (see page 42).

SEASONED FLOUR. Flour mixed with salt and pepper in the proportion of one level tablespoonful salt and ¼ level teaspoon pepper to each 4 oz. flour.

SIFT. To put through a sieve or flour sifter. This is done to remove lumps and, in the case of flour and raising agents, to blend them and mix in air.

SIMMERING. Cooking food below boiling temperature, at 185° F. A liquid simmers when only an occasional bubble shows on the surface. Foods which must be simmered are meat, fish, poultry and stews. Boiling toughens them. (See also "Boiling", page 10.)

SKEWER. A metal or wooden pin used for fastening pieces of meat together and for trussing poultry.

SOUSING. Cooking food slowly in vinegar and spices.

STEAMING. This means simply cooking in steam, either with the food in direct contact with the steam or by having the food in a basin or other dish placed in steam or boiling water. For methods of steaming see the following sections: how to Steam Fish (page 32). Steaming Vegetables (page 51). How to Steam a Pudding (page 79).

STEEP. To soak in hot or cold liquid.

STEWING. This means simmering food, generally meat, fish, poultry or game, in a little liquid. Never let a stew boil. Only an occasional bubble should show on the surface of the liquid. Be careful not to add too much liquid. A stew should be thick, not like a soup. Stews may be cooked on the top of the stove in a saucepan with a tightly fitting lid or in a covered dish or casserole in the oven (see page 41).

STOCK. A well-flavoured liquid made from meat, vegetables or fish and used as a foundation for soups, sauces, stews, etc. (see page 63).

TEMPERATURE. The degree of heat. In cooking the temperature is generally measured in degrees Fahrenheit, expressed as ° F.

Boiling water	212° F.
Simmering water	185° F.
Tepid water	80° F.

For temperatures used in Fat and Sugar cooking, see pages 62 and 73; for baking temperatures see below and page 86.

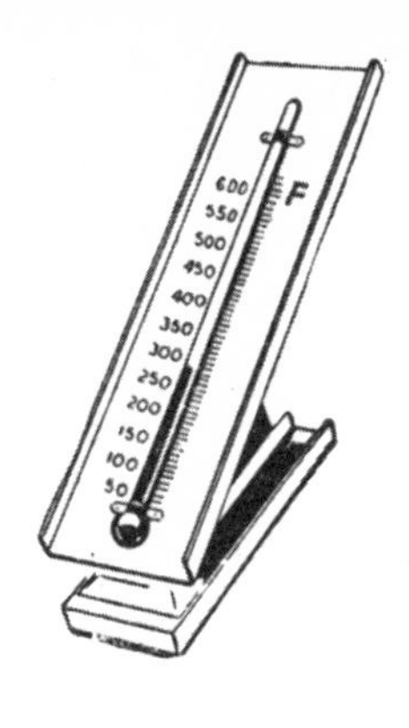

OVEN TEMPERATURE

Oven Temperatures

Most modern stoves are either fitted with a thermometer or an automatic heat control. In all cases the temperatures recommended by the manufacturers should be used. If the oven is not fitted with a temperature indicator of some sort try to obtain an oven thermometer. Guessing is only safe for the very experienced. An oven thermometer should be stood on a shelf in the centre of the oven and the heat adjusted until the thermometer remains steady at the required temperature.

Oven Temperatures Using a Thermometer

If possible use the temperature recommended with individual recipes, or follow the chart supplied with your cooker. The following is a general guide: (see also page 86.)

Slow 250° F. – 350° F.
Egg dishes, Meringues, Oven Stews, Oven Stewed Fruit, Milk Pudding, Rich Fruit Cake, Slow Roasting, Soup or Stock.

Moderate 350° F. – 400° F.
Baked custards, Biscuits, Braising, Cheese dishes, Gingerbread, Large Cake, Plain Fruit Cake, Roast Meat, Souffles, Sponges (fresh eggs).

Moderately Hot 400° F. – 450° F.
Bread, Baked Fish, Baked Potatoes, Layer Cakes, Small Cakes, Victoria Sandwich, Drop Cakes, Sponges (dried egg).

Hot 450° F. – 475° F.
Choux Pastry, Roast Potatoes, Pies, Tarts, Short Pastry, Yeast Rolls.

Very Hot 475° F. – 500° F.
Puff Pastry, Scones, Searing Meat, Flaky Pastry, Yorkshire Pudding.

TEPID. The temperature of a mixture of 2 parts of cold water to 1 part of boiling water, about 80° F.

WHIP. See "Beat". Whipping generally refers to beating cream or eggs (see page 26).

ZEST. The thin outer skin of oranges or lemons. This is the only part which should be used for flavouring as the white pith underneath is so very bitter.

4 *Using Recipes*

Only an experienced cook can follow successfully a carelessly compiled recipe. Many recipes, unfortunately, leave a lot to the imagination or common sense; this means that their lack of precision must be compensated for by experience on the part of the cook. Before trying out a new recipe, be quite sure that you are clear on the following points; otherwise your time and ingredients may easily be wasted and your temper will certainly suffer.

1. Are quantities exactly specified? If these are expressed in cups, spoonfuls, etc., instead of lb. and oz., is the size of the measure clear? Further, is the measure to be filled level, rounded or heaped?
2. Are quantities of all ingredients specified and is it clear what has to be done with each of them? If any quantity of, e.g., a liquid, must be left indefinite, does the recipe say so?
3. Is it clear how many portions are to be expected?
4. In recipes for cakes or biscuits, is the size of the tin or cutter given? Are cooking times and temperatures clear? Although times cannot always be exact, a general indication should always be given.

Unless you are quite sure of these points, you are running the risk of failure.

How to Weigh and Measure

It is most important to weigh or measure all ingredients accurately, especially when making cakes, biscuits, pastry, bread, scones and sauces. There are cooks who seem to be able to produce good results by guesswork but they are generally people who have long experience of cooking, and have learnt by bitter experience and many failures. The only way to be certain of repeating good results and avoiding failures is to be careful with weights and measures every time. You will not find a professional baker guessing. His job depends on the reliability of his results.

Weighing is more accurate than measuring but it is essential to have good scales, preferably Government stamped. The outlay may seem large but it is worth while saving up to buy a good pair of scales as they should last a lifetime. The type which has separate weights lasts longer and is more accurate than the spring-balance type with the weights marked on a dial.

To Weigh

Place the required weight in one pan and the food in the other. When the correct weight of food is in the pan it should see-saw up and down and not be down permanently one side or the other. To weigh sticky things like syrup and fat sprinkle the pan lightly with flour before adding the food.

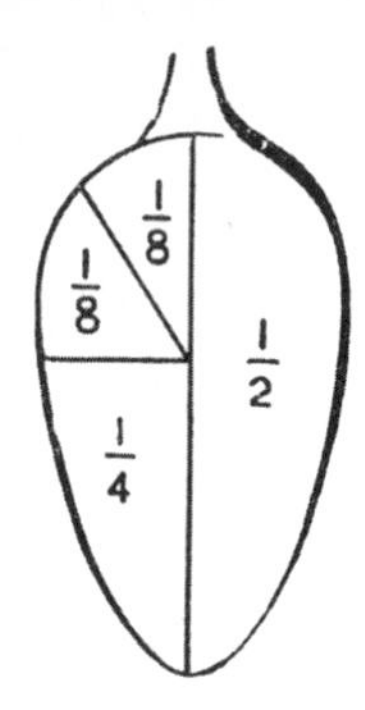

To Measure

The only accurate way of measuring is to use level measures, *i.e., level off to the top of the measure or spoon with a knife.* A heaped spoonful can contain anything from two to four times as much as a level spoonful. To measure half a level spoon divide lengthwise, for a quarter divide the half across the spoon, and for an eighth divide the quarter diagonally.

LEVEL ROUNDED HEAPED

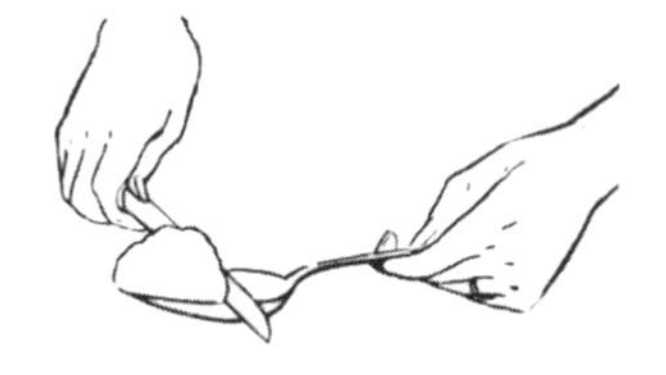

LEVELLING

Table of Weights of Handy Measures

N.B. — These weights are only approximate and vary with the way the spoon or measure is packed. The cup used is a half-pint breakfast cup or measure. A straight sided cup or measure is the best to use as it is very difficult to measure halves and quarters with a cup that tapers. The tablespoon is the size given on the next page.

Food	*Weight of one level half pint*	*Weight of one level tablespoon*
Bacon, chopped	5 oz.	½ oz.
Breadcrumbs, fresh	3 oz.	¼ oz.
Breadcrumbs, dry, sifted	6 oz.	⅓ oz.
Bread, soaked and squeezed	7 oz.	¾ oz.
Cabbage, cooked, shredded	3½ oz.	¼ oz.
Cabbage, raw shredded	2 oz.	⅕ oz.
Carrots, raw sliced	6 oz.	½ oz.
Carrots, raw coarsely grated	5 oz.	¼ oz.
Carrots, cooked diced	6 oz.	½ oz.
Cheese, grated	4 oz.	¼ oz.
Cocoa	5 oz.	¼ oz.
Cornflour	5 oz.	¼ oz.
Custard powder	5 oz.	¼ oz.
Flour, National, unsifted	6 oz.	⅓ oz.
Golden Syrup or Treacle	1 lb.	1 oz.
Haricot Beans	8 oz.	¾ oz.
Jam	12 oz.	1 oz.

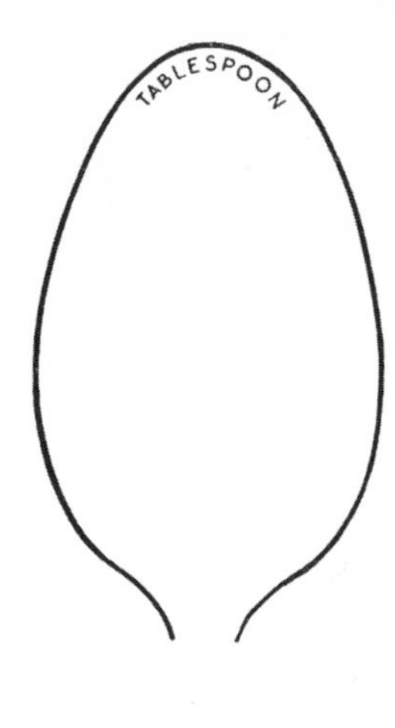

Lard	9 oz.	1 oz.
Lentils	9 oz.	¾ oz.
Margarine	7 oz.	¾ oz.
Minced Beef	8 oz.	½ oz.
Oatmeal, medium	8 oz.	¾ oz.
Oatmeal, coarse	6½ oz.	½ oz.
Oats, rolled or Quaker	5 oz.	¼ oz.
Peas, dried	10 oz.	½ oz.
Potato, cooked mashed	8 oz.	1 oz.
Potato, finely grated raw	11 oz.	1 oz.
Potato, coarsely grated raw	8 oz.	¾ oz.
Prunes, stoned and chopped	6½ oz.	½ oz.
Raisins	6½ oz.	½ oz.
Rice	9 oz.	1 oz.
Semolina	9 oz.	½ oz.
Sugar, granulated	10 oz.	½ oz.
Sultanas	7 oz.	½ oz.

OTHER HANDY MEASURES

1 gill = ¼ pint = approximately 7 level tablespoons
4 gills = 1 pint
2 pints = 1 quart
4 quarts = 1 gallon

5 *How to Season Food*

To know how to season food properly is just as important as to know the right way to boil, bake or fry. Proper seasoning makes good cooking into first-class cooking and dull dishes into exciting ones. Seasonings and flavourings are used to enhance the natural flavour of the food and should be added before or during the cooking process. This ensures that the flavours will be well blended. One exception to this rule is grilled meat when salt should not be added before or during cooking as it tends to draw out the meat juices.

Seasonings have little or no nutritive value, but they are valuable nevertheless because they give variety to dishes and make them more appetising and therefore more readily digested.

The use of seasonings and flavourings is not extravagant for only small amounts are needed. Spices, dried herbs, pepper, mustard, etc., should always be kept in airtight jars or tins or the flavours will deteriorate.

Small amounts of the following spices, dried herbs and seasonings should be kept in every store cupboard, and every cook should try to grow some fresh herbs. Parsley, chives, mint, etc., will grow quite well in pots or window boxes.

Seasoning	*Kinds*
Bay Leaves In a bouquet garni (see page 11) and in soups, stews and sauces.	Fresh or dried
Capers In sauces, salads, sandwich spreads.	Bottled in vinegar or use bottled nasturtium seeds
Cayenne Pepper In savoury dishes. It is much stronger than ordinary pepper.	Ground
Celery Seed In soups, stews and savoury dishes when celery is out of season.	Dried
Chillies These are very hot and are used sparingly in sauces, pickles, stews and savoury rice dishes.	Dried
Chives In place of onion in salads, omelettes and other egg dishes, mashed potatoes, soups and stews.	Fresh from the garden
Cinnamon In cakes, puddings, sauces, stews and savoury dishes.	Ground or stick
Cloves In fruit pies, puddings, cakes, stews, soups.	Whole or ground
Curry Powder In curries and small amounts in scrambled egg, sandwich fillings, stews and soups.	Ground
Essences A great variety of flavours can be achieved by using different essences in puddings and cakes. Try vanilla in coffee and chocolate flavoured foods; almond essence in custard to serve with plums; lemon essence with apple.	In bottles
Garlic Very small amounts in savoury dishes, ¼ or ½ a small clove is sufficient to flavour a soup or stew for four.	As bulbs. Each bulb is made up of many "cloves"
Ginger	
Sliced in cakes, puddings and stewed fruit.	Crystallized
In cakes, puddings, sauces, stews and savoury dishes.	Ground
In sweet and savoury dishes but is removed before serving.	Whole pickling (root)
Horseradish In a sauce with roast beef or fish and grated in sandwich spreads and savoury dishes.	Fresh root or bottled, grated
Lemons In fish dishes, stuffings, stews, sauces, cakes and puddings.	Fresh fruit, dried peel or juice
Mace In sweet and savoury sauces, cakes, puddings, potatoes, spinach, stuffings, stews and fish stock.	Ground or whole in "blades"

Seasoning	*Kinds*
Marjoram In sauces, stews, soups, rissoles and other savoury dishes.	Dried or fresh
Mint In sauces; with vegetables during cooking; in sweet tarts; in stuffings for lamb; and in salads and sandwich fillings.	Fresh or dried
Mustard The seed is generally only used in pickles and chutneys. Ground mustard may be used in all savoury dishes.	Ground or whole mustard seed
Nutmeg Use in the same way as mace or grated on top of milk puddings, custards and junkets.	Whole or ground
Onions In all savoury dishes.	Fresh or dried
Orange In savoury dishes, cakes, pies, puddings and sauces.	Whole, fresh or dried rind
Paprika For sprinkling on dishes to add colour and for flavouring. Used in making goulash.	Ground red pepper less pungent than cayenne)
Parsley In all savoury dishes.	Fresh or dried (fresh is better)
Pepper In all savoury dishes. Home ground pepper has the best flavour.	Whole peppercorns or ground
Sage In savoury dishes and stuffings but especially with duck, pork and goose.	Fresh or dried
Salt In all savoury dishes. A little in all sweet dishes, cakes, etc., improves the flavour.	Cooking
Sugar In all sweet dishes. A little in savoury dishes brings out the other flavours.	Any
Thyme In stuffings and savoury dishes.	Fresh or dried
Vinegar A little added to stews, sauces or other savoury dishes often improves the flavour. Vinegar helps to make meat more tender.	Malt, Tarragon, Chilli, Garlic, Wine, Elderflower, etc.

6 *Milk and Cheese*

Milk

Cow's milk is sold fresh, dried, evaporated and condensed. All these types of milk are used in cookery.

Some Ways of Using Milk in the Menu

It is most important, especially for children, that plenty of milk should be included in the menu. There are many ways of using it besides as a beverage; for example, in sauces, sweet and savoury; in cream soups; in cocoa; in puddings such as rice pudding, custards, cornflour moulds and junket; in batters, pancakes and fritters, and in mixing scones, cakes and buns.

Fresh Milk

Milk can be the means of spreading diseases such as tuberculosis, diphtheria and scarlet fever, so it is important to buy milk produced under hygienic conditions. Unless milk has come from a herd of tuberculin tested cows or has been pasteurized, it should be scalded or boiled before drinking.

To Scald Milk

Heat it gently in an uncovered pan until bubbles begin to appear round the edges. It is better to do this in a double boiler or in a basin over a pan of water for milk burns easily. After scalding, pour the milk into a clean jug and cool quickly by standing the jug in a bowl of cold water.

Keeping Milk Fresh

1. Keep in a cool place and in hot weather stand the jug or bottle in a bowl of cold water with a piece of muslin over the top. Have the ends of the cloth resting in the water. Stand in a draught.
2. See that all jugs are kept clean. Wash in cold water first, then in very hot water and give a final rinse in cold water. Do not wipe with a used cloth.
3. Always keep milk covered from dust and flies and away from foods which have a strong smell.
4. Do not mix new milk with old unless it is to be used at once.

Dried Milk

Dried Milk is milk with the water removed. It may be made from whole or from skim milk, which is milk with the cream removed. National Household Milk is dried skim milk.

1. Mix dried milk according to the directions on the container. After mixing it will not keep any longer than fresh milk.
2. Dried milk burns very easily. To avoid burning sauces, milk puddings, etc., do not reconstitute the milk but make the recipe with water and add the milk, mixed to a paste, at the end.
3. When using dried milk in cakes, puddings, and batters, there is no need to reconstitute it. Add it dry with the dry ingredients and mix the whole with water.
4. Dried milk mixed to a thick paste with water, sweetened, flavoured and beaten well makes a very good substitute for cream.
5. Store dried milk in a cool place away from foods which have a strong smell.

Evaporated Milk

Evaporated Milk is milk with some of the water removed so that it is thicker than fresh milk. It should be thinned down according to the directions on the tin. Generally an equal amount of water is added. Then treat as fresh milk. After the tin has been opened evaporated milk will not keep any longer than fresh milk.

Condensed Milk

Condensed Milk is evaporated milk with added sugar. Mix according to the directions on the tin and use in place of fresh milk in cooking, making allowance for the sweetening. Condensed milk will keep two or three days after the tin has been opened, as the sugar helps to preserve it.

Sour Milk

Milk sours because it contains bacteria which feed on the sugar in the milk and form an acid, called lactic acid. The acid makes the milk form a clot. A similar clot is formed when rennet is added to milk to make junket but the sour taste is absent. The solid clot is called "curd" and the liquid which separates out is called "whey".

Sour milk should not be wasted but it is better to use it in cooked dishes as the conditions which bring about the souring also encourage the growth of any harmful bacteria which may be present. Cooking will destroy these bacteria so use the milk in mixing cakes, scones and puddings. The curd may be used in making fillings for tarts, in which case use the whey for mixing cakes, etc.

Milk which has been pasteurized or boiled will not sour generally as readily as fresh milk, but it may be used for making junket provided it is lukewarm before the rennet is added.

Cheese

For cooking purposes the harder cheeses are the best to use. Parmesan cheese or a dry Cheddar cheese will grate more finely than the softer cheeses and is better for cooking. A supply of ready grated cheese can be kept in an airtight bottle or jar, provided the cheese is thoroughly dry before storing. Cheese which is not grated should be wrapped in greased paper and hung in a piece of muslin in a cool, airy place.

Cooking Cheese

When cheese is heated it melts at a fairly low temperature and if the heat is increased beyond this the cheese becomes tough and stringy. It is, therefore, better to cook cheese dishes at a fairly low temperature or if they must be cooked at a high temperature the cooking should be for as short a time as possible.

Making Cheese Sauce

Make the sauce first and when it is cooked add the grated cheese and heat gently, without boiling, until the cheese melts and blends smoothly. This will give a much better result than if the sauce is allowed to boil after adding the cheese.

Some Ways of Using Grated Cheese

1. In cheese sauce with vegetables.
2. Mixed with browned breadcrumbs and fat and sprinkled on the top of cooked vegetables. Brown under the grill or in a hot oven.
3. With salads and sandwich fillings.
4. In omelettes and scrambled eggs.
5. Sprinkled on the top of vegetable soups.
6. In savoury dishes with rice, spaghetti, macaroni, etc.

7 *Eggs*

Hen eggs are those most commonly used in cooking although duck eggs and goose eggs may sometimes be used. Hen eggs are sold in the shell or dried. Dried eggs are eggs with only the shell and water removed.

Storing Eggs

SHELL EGGS should be wiped clean if necessary and stored in a cool, dry place. Eggs readily absorb odours and should not be kept near strong smelling foods. To preserve eggs for several months, use water-glass or one of the special egg preservatives, following the directions given on the container.

DRIED EGGS should be kept in a cool, dry place away from foods which have a strong odour. They should not be kept in a refrigerator. An opened packet should keep for three weeks and an unopened packet for three months but this depends on how long the packets were stored before they were sold.

The Effect of Heat on Eggs

An egg sets or coagulates at a temperature of 160° F., which is lower than the temperature of boiling water (see page 16). When heated above this temperature it becomes hard and tough. For this reason eggs, whenever possible, should be cooked slowly, especially when boiled, poached, scrambled or made into custards (see pages 27–28).

When shell eggs are added to sauces or hot milk the liquid should not be allowed to boil after the eggs have been added or they may set quickly in small, hard flakes which give a curdled appearance to the sauce or milk.

How to Prepare Shell Eggs for Cooking

Break each egg separately into a small bowl or cup to make sure it is fresh before adding it to the mixture. The easiest way to break an egg is to hold it in the left hand and tap it with a knife; then put the thumbs into the crack and break the shell apart. If the white and yolk are to be separated tip the yolk carefully from one half of the shell to the other until all the white has fallen into the basin below.

How to Prepare Dried Eggs for Cooking

RECONSTITUTING. One level tablespoon of dried egg plus 2 tablespoons of water equals 1 fresh egg. It is very important to be careful with the mixing and reconstitution of dried eggs to make sure that the mixture is smooth and free from lumps. If the egg is very lumpy, rub it through a fine sieve before mixing. Then add just enough water to make a thick mixture and beat very thoroughly until quite smooth. Add the remaining water and mix well. After mixing, dried eggs will not keep any longer than broken fresh eggs and should be used up quickly.

DRIED EGGS USED DRY. It is not always necessary to reconstitute dried eggs before use. When they are being used in batters, plain cakes, pastry, flour and egg custards or sauces, the eggs may be mixed dry with the flour or other dry ingredients and the water needed for reconstitution added with the other liquid in the recipe.

When making a cake by the creaming method (see page 76) dried eggs may be beaten dry into the fat and sugar and the water beaten in gradually afterwards. If there are more than 2 eggs in the recipe, add only half the water during creaming, and add the rest with the flour.

ROTARY BEATER

WIRE WHISK

How to Beat Eggs

Fresh eggs beat up more easily and to a greater volume than dried eggs and for this reason they generally make more satisfactory sponges, souffles, choux pastry and similar dishes.

Beating is very much easier if the right shaped bowl is used for the beater.

1. For the rotary beater it is better to use a deep, narrow basin in order that the thick part of the beater may be covered by the egg.

2. For a wire egg whisk it is better to use a wide bowl. One or two egg whites can be very easily beaten on a flat plate, using a table fork or knife.

How to Boil Shell Eggs

1. Bring the water to the boil in a saucepan, using enough water to cover the eggs.

2. When the water is boiling, lower the eggs carefully into the pan, using a spoon.

3. Cover and boil gently for the required time. Take care not to race the boiling or the eggs may crack. A new-laid egg requires 3–3½ minutes to be lightly cooked, 4–5 minutes to be moderately soft; 10 minutes to be hard boiled. Less time is required for eggs which are not so fresh.

4. Crack the shells of hard-boiled eggs, to be served cold, as soon as they are cooked and plunge them into cold water. Leave to cool. This helps to avoid a dark ring round the yolk, which is often the result of over-cooking.

Coddled Eggs

These are generally considered more digestible than boiled eggs in which the white is sometimes liable to be tough. Boil the water as before, add the eggs and cover the pan. Turn down the heat so that the water is hot but not boiling.

Leave 4 minutes for a soft-cooked egg, 6–7 minutes for a medium-cooked egg, 15–20 minutes for a hard-boiled egg.

How to Hard Boil Dried Eggs

Reconstitute the eggs, season well and pour them into small greased moulds or egg cups. Stand these in a saucepan with boiling water coming half-way up the sides of the moulds and simmer until the eggs are set, about 15–20 minutes. Turn out of the moulds and use as required.

How to Poach Shell Eggs

1. Fill a frying-pan about half-full of water. There should be enough to cover the eggs. Add 1 level teaspoon of salt to each pint of water, and a tablespoon of vinegar.
2. Bring the water to the boil.
3. Break each egg separately into a saucer (in case it should be bad) and slide it gently into the water.
4. Turn down the heat so that the water no longer boils.
5. Leave 5 minutes or until the egg is lightly set, that is, when the white becomes opaque.
6. Lift out with a fish slice, drain and serve on toast.

N.B. — *Seasoned reconstituted dried eggs may be cooked in an egg poacher when they will be similar to a savoury egg custard.*

How to Scramble Eggs

Whether using fresh or dried eggs the method is the same.

1. Beat the eggs to mix well, allowing 1 to 2 eggs per person.
2. Add seasoning and 1 tablespoon of milk for each egg.
3. Heat enough margarine or butter in a pan to cover the bottom and when melted but not hot add the eggs.
4. Cook slowly over a very gentle heat until just set. Do not stir the eggs more than is necessary to keep them from sticking to the pan. The cooking may be done in a double boiler or a basin over a saucepan of boiling water.
5. Serve when they are just set. If over-cooked they will become hard and tough with a watery liquid separating out. Time for cooking, about 5 minutes.

How to Make an Omelette

There are many different ways of making an omelette according to individual taste. The following method is recommended as being one of the simplest and it can be used for both shell and dried eggs. It is important to have a perfectly clean, smooth pan or the omelette will stick (see page 5).

1. Mix the eggs thoroughly and add seasoning. Allow 2 to 3 eggs per person.
2. Heat enough fat (butter, clarified dripping, or cooking fat, *not* margarine) to cover the bottom of the pan and when very hot add the eggs. Dripping or cooking fat flavoured with onion is very good for frying savoury omelettes.
3. Cook over a brisk heat, lifting the edges as the omelette sets and allowing the uncooked egg to run underneath. An alternative method is to stir the eggs gently until nearly set but care must be taken not to stir too briskly lest the eggs curdle and also to stop stirring before they are quite set.
4. When the omelette is just set (it takes about 1 minute) but still moist, fold over and serve.
5. If the omelette is to be stuffed, lay the hot cooked filling on top before folding over. Cooked chopped mushroom, bacon, onion, potatoes and so on may be mixed with the egg before cooking.

How to Make Custards with Shell or Dried Eggs

When beaten eggs are mixed with milk and heated gently the eggs thicken the milk, the thickness depending on the proportion of egg to milk and on the method of cooking. A mixture which is stirred during cooking does not set as firmly as one which is cooked without stirring. Custards which are stirred during cooking are called pouring or "boiled" custards (although the mixture should never be allowed to boil or it will curdle). Those which are not stirred are "steamed" or "baked" custards.

All custards are mixed in the following way:

1. Beat the eggs slightly to mix them well.
2. Add the sugar and flavouring and mix well.
3. Heat the milk and pour it gradually on to the eggs and sugar, stirring all the time. Cold milk may be used with shell eggs although the cooking is quicker if hot milk is used. Boiling milk should be used with dried eggs as the cooking must be rapid to give good results.
4. For a pouring custard, cook in a double boiler or in a jug standing in a pan of boiling water. Stir all the time using a wooden spoon. When the custard just coats the back of the spoon it is cooked. This takes 20–30 minutes. Cool immediately.
5. For a baked custard, pour the mixture into a greased dish and stand this in a baking pan with hot water half way up the sides of the dish. Bake in a moderate oven until set. To test, insert a knife and if it comes out clean the custard is set. It takes from 35–60 minutes depending on the size of the custard and whether a shallow or a deep dish has been used. A deep dish takes longer than a shallow one.
6. For a steamed custard, pour the mixture into a greased mould or basin and stand this in a pan of hot water. The water should come two-thirds of the way

up the sides of the dish and should not be allowed to boil. Simmer until the custard is set. Test in the same way as the baked custard. Time as for a baked custard.

7. For a custard tart, pour the hot custard into the unbaked pastry. This method gives better results than using a cold custard. Bake in a hot oven for 40–50 minutes. Test in the same way as a baked custard.

PROPORTIONS

3 to 4 eggs, 1 pint of milk, 1 level tablespoon of sugar, ¼ level teaspoon of salt and vanilla or other flavouring. If desired, more eggs may be used for a baked or steamed custard; the custard will be firmer which is an advantage with certain dishes, for example, caramel custard, or custard tart. *This quantity is sufficient for four helpings.*

8 *Fish*

Fish is sold as fresh, salted, smoked, pickled or canned. It may be further classified as salt water, fresh water, or shell fish.

The following list includes the fish most commonly sold by fishmongers but it is by no means a complete list of edible fish. When buying fish which is unfamiliar ask the fishmonger's advice as to the best method of cooking it.

Name of Fish		*Best Methods of Serving*
COD	Fresh	Grilled, fried, boiled, stewed, steamed or baked.
	Salt	Soak 24–48 hours, boil, then combine with other ingredients in fish cakes, pies, etc.
	Smoked	Grilled, boiled, baked or steamed.
CRAB	Fresh	Generally sold cooked. Use in salads, combined with sauces, or in sandwich fillings.
	Canned	Use as fresh.
DAB	Fresh	Boiled, fried, steamed or stewed.
DOG FISH	Fresh	Baked, fried or curried.
EELS	Fresh	Boiled, fried, stewed, jellied and in pies.
	Smoked	No cooking required. Eat cold as hors d'oeuvre or in sandwiches.
FLOUNDER	Fresh	Fried or grilled.
HADDOCK	Fresh	Boiled, steamed, stewed, baked or fried.
	Smoked	Boiled, baked or grilled.
HALIBUT	Fresh	Grilled, fried, boiled, baked, stewed or steamed.
HAKE	Fresh	Fried, boiled, baked or stewed.
HERRING	Fresh	Boiled, steamed, stewed, fried, baked, soused or grilled.
	Salt	Soak in cold water 12 hours, then use as a fresh herring, use raw as hors d'oeuvre or in salads.
	Kipper	Fried, grilled, baked or stewed in a frying-pan in a little milk and water.
	Bloater	Grilled or fried.

Name of Fish		*Best Methods of Serving*
LOBSTER	Fresh	Generally sold cooked. Use in salads combined with sauces, or in sandwich fillings.
	Canned	Use as fresh.
MACKEREL	Fresh	Steamed, boiled, baked, soused, grilled or fried.
	Smoked	Grilled or fried.
	Canned	In salads, fish cakes and combined with sauces.
MULLET	Fresh	Boiled, grilled, stewed, steamed or fried.
MUSSEL	Fresh	Boiled, fried soups or stews.
	Bottled	In hors d'oeuvre, soups or stews.
PILCHARDS	Canned	Salads, sandwich fillings, fish cakes, etc.
PLAICE	Fresh	Boiled, fried, steamed, stewed or grilled.
PRAWNS	Fresh	Generally sold cooked. Use in hors d'oeuvre, salads, and curried.
	Canned	Use as fresh.
SALMON	Fresh	Boiled, steamed, fried or grilled.
	Canned	In salads, sandwich fillings, fish cakes, and combined with sauces.
	Smoked	In hors d'oeuvre, salads and sandwiches.
SCALLOPS	Fresh	Fried or creamed.
SKATE or RAY	Fresh	Steamed, boiled or fried.
SOLE	Fresh	Boiled, stewed, steamed, fried or grilled.
SPRATS	Fresh	Fried or grilled.
	Smoked	Grilled or uncooked as hors d'oeuvre.
TURBOT	Fresh	Grilled, boiled, steamed, stewed or fried.
WHITEBAIT	Fresh	Fried.
WHITING	Fresh	Boiled, steamed, stewed, fried or baked.

Buying Fresh Fish

It is most important that fish should be very fresh. It goes bad very quickly and should be cooked as soon as possible.

The following are points to look for when buying fresh fish:
1. The gills should be bright and clear.
2. The eyes should be full and bright, not sunken and dull.
3. The flesh should be firm and the tail straight, not drooping.
4. There should be no disagreeable odour.

How to Prepare Fish for Cooking

TO SCALE use the back of a knife and, holding the fish by the tail, scrape firmly from the tail towards the head. Wash well to remove loose scales.

TO CLEAN

a) **Round Fish**, such as herrings, whiting, mackerel, etc. Slit the belly from the head

towards the vent, remove all the entrails, keeping the roe. Wash well. If desired, the head may be removed

b) **Flat Fish**, such as sole, flounder, dab, etc. The belly is just behind the head. Cut away the gills and make a small opening in the belly. Pull out the gut and wash the fish well. If the head is to be removed do this with a semi-circular cut at the base of the head.

TO FILLET. Slit the fish down the backbone and with a sharp knife separate the flesh from the backbone on each side. Use the bones and trimmings for fish stock or soup (see page 63).

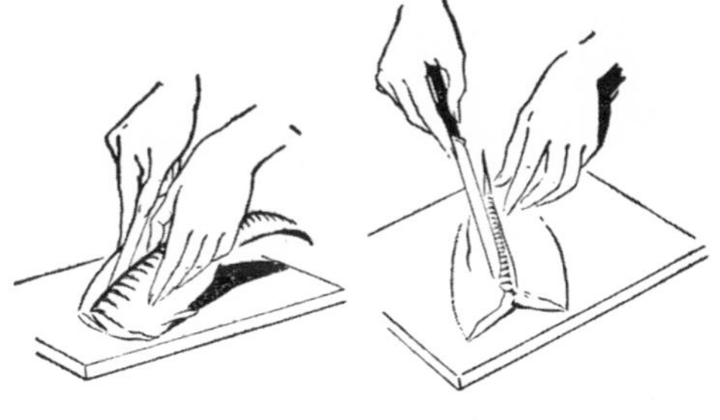

FILLETING ROUND AND FLAT FISH

How to Boil Fish

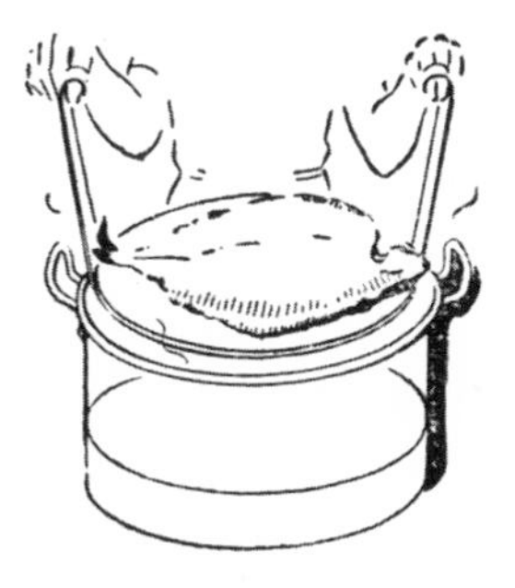

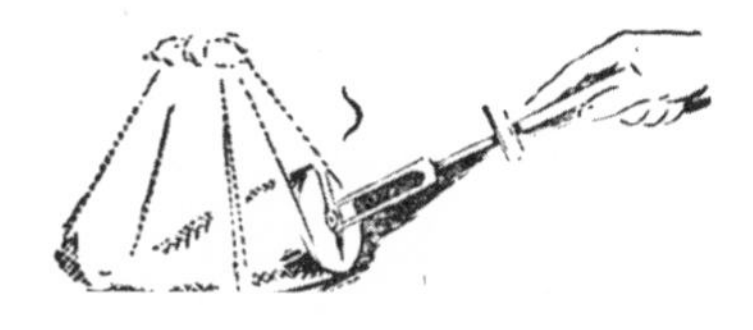

1. Do not use more water than is needed just to cover the fish.
2. Boil the water and to each quart add 1 tablespoon vinegar, 2 level teaspoons of salt and 3 peppercorns. For additional flavouring add a bouquet garni (see page 11), and 1 carrot and 1 onion. This will help to give a well-flavoured stock to use for a sauce to serve with the fish or for fish soup.
3. When the water is boiling add the fish. Cover the pan and immediately reduce the temperature and simmer gently for the required time (see below). The fish is more easily handled if placed on a metal steaming rack before being put in the boiling water, or tied loosely in clean muslin.
4. Fish is cooked when the flesh separates easily from the bone. Test at the thickest part, or if there is no bone it is cooked when a white creamy substance begins to run from the fish.
5. Drain very thoroughly, serve with parsley, caper or anchovy sauce made from the fish stock.

Boiling Time-table for Fish

Thin fish, 7 minutes per lb., plus 7 minutes.
Thick fish, 10 minutes per lb., plus 10 minutes.

EXAMPLE. A thin fish weighing 2 lb. needs 2 by 7 minutes, plus another 7 minutes, or 21 minutes in all.

How to Steam Fish

METHOD A. Place the fish in the steamer, sprinkle with salt and cook until the flesh will leave the bones easily. Test at the thickest part (see page 31). If the fish is large, turn once during steaming. Times as for boiling.

METHOD B. Cut the fish in convenient pieces for serving and place in a well-greased soup plate. Sprinkle with salt, and if liked, with a little milk. Place the soup plate over a pan of boiling water or cooking potatoes and put the saucepan lid or an inverted plate on top. Steam 10–15 minutes. Serve with parsley, anchovy, caper or tomato sauce and boiled potatoes.

How to Grill Fish

(See also page 14)

1. Heat the grill and grease the grid or grill rack.
2. Small whole fish should be cut across in deep gashes to allow the heat to penetrate. Otherwise the outside of the fish will dry up before the inside is cooked.

Cutlets and white fish will need basting with melted fat.

3. Grill the fish until the flesh easily leaves the bones (see page 31) when tested with a fork. Serve at once. If possible serve Tartare sauce or brown butter sauce or parsley butter with the fish. Garnish with watercress.

How to Fry Fish

(See "Fats and Oils", page 58)

How to Bake Fish

1. This method is most satisfactory if moderate sized whole fish are used. Scale and clean but leave the head and tail on.

2. Stuff the belly with a savoury forcemeat and sew up with a needle and coarse thread. Do not fill the fish too tightly or it will burst during cooking because the stuffing swells as it cooks.
3. The fish may be skewered into the form of a letter S as though it were swimming.
4. Place the fish in a baking pan with a little fat and bake in a moderately hot oven until the flesh easily leaves the bones (see page 31). For a fish weighing up to 4 lb. allow 10 minutes per lb. and 5 minutes for each additional lb., although the time required depends very largely on the thickness of the fish.
5. To serve, remove the skewer and thread and garnish with parsley and lemon. Serve with a tomato or a sharp sauce.

Fish may be baked as above without the stuffing.

How to Stew Fish

1. Place the fish in a saucepan or casserole with just enough fish stock (see page 63), milk or water to moisten. Season.
2. Cover and simmer very gently until the flesh easily leaves the bones (see page 31). The cooking may be carried out on top of the stove or in the oven. For times, see "How to Boil Fish", page 31.
3. Flavour and thicken the liquid and serve it as a sauce. For sauces, see page 65.

Using Up Cooked or Canned Fish

Use in salads, sandwich fillings, fish cakes, kedgeree, pies and combined with sauces or creamed.

As with all reheated foods care should be taken to season well and to see that the fish is warmed through without being over-heated or twice cooked.

How to Carve Whole Fish

Use a fish knife or a large flat knife or spoon. Work along the backbone of the fish, lifting the flesh first off one side and then the other. In this way the fish can be served free from bones.

What to Serve with Fish

Fried or grilled fish

Potatoes	Fried or boiled
Vegetables	Green salad, coleslaw, green peas or beans, carrots, tomatoes, parsnips.

Sauces and Accompaniments	Tartare sauce, caper sauce, Hollandaise sauce, tomato sauce, lemon, parsley butter, pickled beetroot or red cabbage, chutney, mustard sauce.
Boiled or steamed	
Potatoes	Boiled, jacket or mashed
Vegetables	Green peas or beans, carrots, tomatoes, spinach, celery, green salad, cucumber salad, parsnips.
Sauces and Accompaniments	Cheese sauce, horseradish sauce, chutney sauce, lemon sauce, parsley sauce, egg sauce, fennel sauce, anchovy sauce, Hollandaise sauce.
Baked	
Potatoes	Baked or boiled
Vegetables	Green peas or beans, carrots, green salad, tomatoes, cucumber salad, spinach, celery, parsnips.
Sauces and Accompaniments	Tomato sauce, brown sauce, Tartare sauce, caper sauce, lemon, parsley butter, anchovy sauce, Hollandaise sauce, mustard sauce.

9 *Meat, Game and Poultry*

MEAT includes beef, veal, mutton, lamb, pork and offal or meat sundries such as heart, sweetbread, liver, kidney, brains, etc.

GAME includes wild animals such as deer, rabbit and hares and wild birds such as pheasant, quail, partridges, grouse, etc. Rabbit and hare are the most widely used and will be the only ones dealt with here.

POULTRY includes chickens, turkeys, ducks and geese.

What Good Meat Looks Like

BEEF should be bright red, fine grained, firm and elastic to the touch and well marked or marbled with fine, cream-coloured fat. Poor quality beef is flabby, dark and coarse with yellow fat.

Beef from an old or under-fed animal has very little fat.

VEAL should be pale pink with clear, firm white fat.

LAMB should be red with white fat. The bones should be moist and red at the joints.

MUTTON should be bright red with yellowish fat, having a waxy appearance. The bones are white.

PORK should be pale brownish red and the flesh firm. The fat should be white and firm.

Why Meat is Cooked

1. To improve the flavour. Meat contains substances called "extractives" which, when the meat is cooked, give it a characteristic pleasant flavour most pronounced with grilled, fried and roasted meats.
2. To improve the appearance.

MEAT FIBRES

3. To make it tender. Meat consists of bundles of long fibres or cells bound together by a tough substance called connective tissue. Tough meat has more connective tissue than tender meat and meat from the legs and neck of an animal where the muscles are used a great deal has more connective tissue than other parts and is therefore tougher. Meat from old animals has more connective tissue than meat from young animals. Tough cuts of meat need cooking for a long time at a low moist temperature to soften the connective tissue and make the meat tender, for example, by stewing (page 41), boiling (page 40) or braising (page 44). An alternative method of making tough meat tender is to mince it and so break up the connective tissue.

Meat from a freshly killed animal is tougher than meat which has been hung for some time. Very soon after killing the muscles of an animal become tough and hard but if the meat is hung for some days the muscles soften again owing to the action of acids formed in the meat. Vinegar contains acid, and if it is added to meat before cooking (see "Marinade", page 14) or during cooking it helps to make it more tender. Tomatoes, lemon juice or wine added to a stew have much the same effect.

Cuts of Meat and Their Uses

Cuts vary in different parts of the country and with different butchers, but the following list gives the more common names.

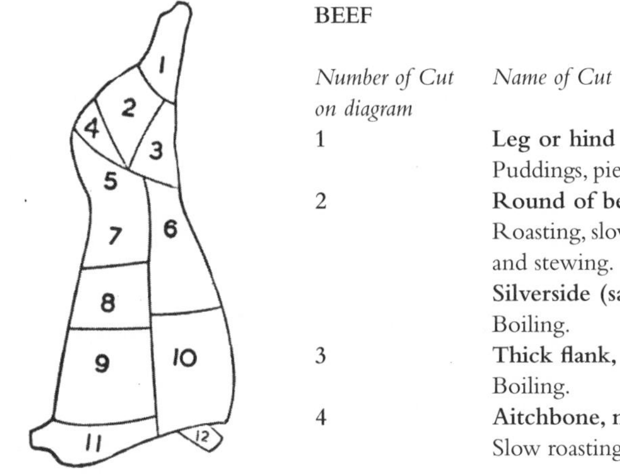

BEEF

Number of Cut on diagram	*Name of Cut*
1	**Leg or hind shin** Puddings, pies, stews, soups and braising.
2	**Round of beef, top rump or top side** Roasting, slow roasting, braising or top side and stewing.
	Silverside (salted) Boiling.
3	**Thick flank, bed piece, first cutting, or brail** Boiling.
4	**Aitchbone, middle rump, or shell bone** Slow roasting, boiling, salting.

Number of Cut on diagram	*Name of Cut*
5	**Rump, fillet, hip or pin bone steak.** Frying and grilling.
6	**Flank or skirt** Braising, boiling, stewing, pies and puddings and slow roasting.
7	**Sirloin** Roasting.
8	**Fore ribs, standing ribs, wing rib, or best chine** Roasting.
9	**Middle ribs, back and top ribs, shoulder piece, or chuck ribs** Slow roasting, braising.
10	**Brisket or plate, fresh** Stewing, boiling, slow roasting and braising.
	Brisket, salted Boiling.
11	**Stewing beef may be called neck, clod or sticking piece** Stews, pies, puddings, soups.
12	**Fore shin** Stews, stocks, soups and puddings.

OFFAL AND SUNDRIES

Name	*Uses*	*Name*	*Uses*
Ox Heart	Stewing and braising.	Ox Tongue	Boiling and pressing, often salted.
Ox Tail	Soups, stews and braising.	Ox Brains	Boiling, then sometimes fried.
Ox Kidney	Soups, stews, puddings, and pies.	Tripe	Stewing and braising.
Suet	Stuffings, pastry and rendering for dripping.	Cow Heel	Stewing and braising.

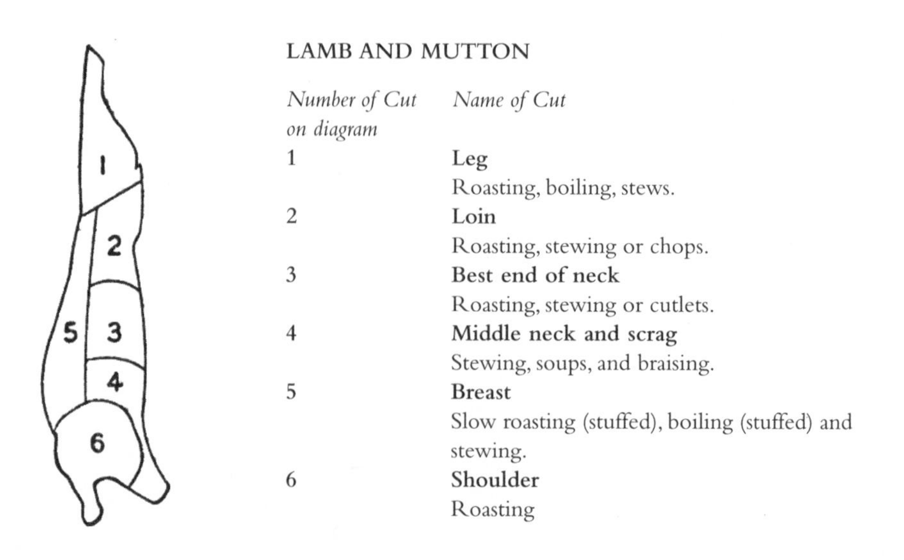

LAMB AND MUTTON

Number of Cut on diagram	*Name of Cut*
1	**Leg** Roasting, boiling, stews.
2	**Loin** Roasting, stewing or chops.
3	**Best end of neck** Roasting, stewing or cutlets.
4	**Middle neck and scrag** Stewing, soups, and braising.
5	**Breast** Slow roasting (stuffed), boiling (stuffed) and stewing.
6	**Shoulder** Roasting

OFFAL AND SUNDRIES

Name	*Uses*	*Name*	*Uses*
Sheep's head	Braising, broth and stews.	Tongues	Boiling and braising.
Hearts	Stewing, slow roasting (stuffed) and braising.	Brains	Boiling.
		Sweetbreads	Frying.
Kidneys	Frying and grilling.	Trotters	Stewing and braising.

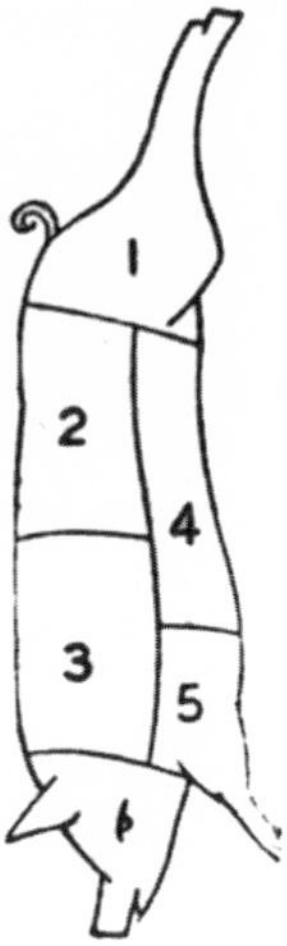

PORK

Number of Cut on diagram	*Name of Cut*
1	**Leg** Boiling and roasting.
2	**Loin** Boiling, roasting or chops.
3	**Spare ribs and best end of neck, or blade bone or fine end** Boiling, slow roasting or chops.
4	**Belly (often salted)** Boiling and stewing.
5	**Hand and spring** Boiling and stewing.
6	**Head (often salted).** Half the head is called "Pig's cheek" Boiling and used in brawn.

OFFAL AND SUNDRIES

Name	*Uses*	*Name*	*Uses*
Trotters and ears	Stewing and used in brawn.	Brains	Boiling and frying.
Tongues	Boiling, braising and used in brawn.	Kidney	Stewing and braising.
		Liver	Frying and baking.

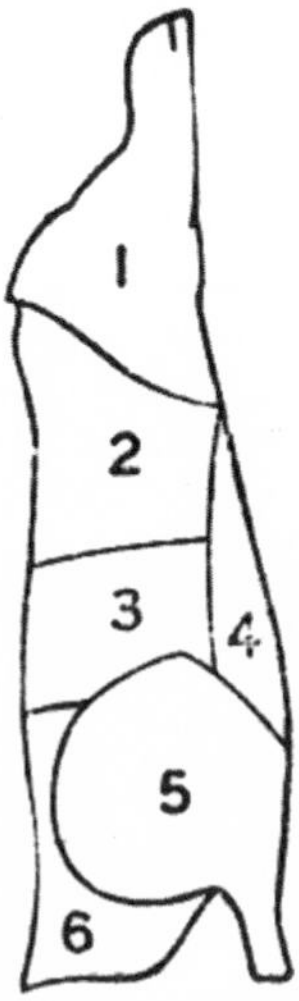

VEAL

Number of Cut on diagram	*Name of Cut*
1	**Leg** Roasting. **Fillet** Frying.
2	**Loin** Roasting or chops.
3	**Best end of neck** Braising, stewing, slow roasting, or cutlets.
4	**Breast** Stewing, braising, slow roasting (stuffed).
5	**Shoulder** Stuffed and roasted, stewed.
6	**Scrag** Stewing and braising.

OFFAL AND SUNDRIES

Name	*Uses*	*Name*	*Uses*
Sweetbreads	Braising, frying, grilling.	Feet	Boiling for jelly or stewed and fried.
Brains	Frying.		
Heart	Slow roasting and braising.	Liver	Fried.
Head	Boiling.	Kidney	Stews and pies.

POULTRY

Chickens	Roasted, or fried if very young.
Fowls	Stewed, boiled, may be steamed and then roasted.
Ducks and Ducklings	Roasted and braised.
Geese	Roasted.
Turkeys	Roasted.

GAME

Rabbits	Roasted, stewed, braised or boiled.
Hares	Stewed and braised, or if young, roasted.

Keeping Meat

Hang the meat in a cool airy place in a muslin meat cover, or place it on a rack on top of a plate with a piece of muslin to cover. Meat should not sit in its own juices.

How to Prepare Meat for Cooking

Fresh meat	Wipe the surface with a damp cloth.
Salted meat	Soak in cold water if very salty.
Brains	Soak in cold salt water until all blood is removed and remove skin and fibres.
Ears, pig's	Soak in cold water 5–6 hours.
Feet, cow-heel	Usually sold prepared for cooking.
Feet, pig's	Wash well.
Lamb's trotter	Wash well.
Calf's feet	Usually sold prepared for cooking.
Head, calf's	Cut in half, remove brains, wash and soak in salted water until all the blood is removed. Change the water several times, then blanch by boiling 15–20 minutes (see page 10).
Pig's cheek	If salted, soak in cold water.
Sheep's head	Wash in several waters and soak 1 hour in salted water. Then blanch (see page 10).
Heart, any	Wash in several waters and leave to soak in cold water for 1 hour. Squeeze out all blood.
Kidneys, any	Remove fat, skin and hard core.
Liver, any	Wash and dry.
Ox-tail	Wash, dry and cut in joints.

Sweetbreads	Soak in cold water for 1 hour to remove the blood. Blanch (see page 10). Lamb's sweetbreads should be just brought to the boil, veal sweetbreads need boiling 10–12 minutes. Leave till cold. Then remove gristle and tissue before finishing the cooking.
Tongue, ox	Salted: soak in cold water 2–3 hours. Unsalted: as fresh meat.
Tongue, sheep's	Soak in salt water for 2 hours, then blanch (see page 10).
Tongue, pig's	Soak in salt water for 2 hours, then blanch.
Tongue, calf's	Boiled with the head.
Tripe	Usually sold prepared for cooking.

How to Prepare Poultry for Cooking

1. Pull out (pluck) all the feathers, being careful not to tear the skin. Remove the pin feathers with a knife, and singe the hairs by holding the bird over a gas flame or a lighted spill or taper.
2. Cut off the head.
3. Pull back the skin of the neck and cut off the neck close to the body. Cook the neck with the giblets (see below). Remove the crop and windpipe and loosen the entrails by working round the body with the forefinger.
4. Break the legs at the lower joint and bend them back. This exposes the tendons which can then be drawn out, taking care not to tear the flesh. To draw out the tendons lever up the exposed part with a skewer and pull. If the tendons are not taken out the leg may be too tough to eat, especially turkey's legs.
5. Lay the bird on its back, cut through the skin just above the vent and loosen the fat. Cut out the vent.
6. Loosen all the entrails before attempting to draw them out, thus avoiding breaking them. To do this hold the bird firmly with the left hand and insert the right hand carefully between the inside walls of the body and the membrane holding the entrails together.
7. Take hold of the gizzard and draw the entrails out, being careful not to break the gall bladder or liver.
8. Be sure the lungs and kidneys are removed from the hollows by the backbone.
9. Wash the inside thoroughly in running cold water.

How to Clean the Giblets (Heart, Liver, Gizzard and Feet)

1. Cut through the thick muscle of the gizzard and peel it off the lining. Discard the lining and contents.
2. Cut the heart open.
3. Remove the gall bladder very carefully from the liver. Scald the feet in boiling water for a minute or two and then pull off the skin.
4. Wash all the giblets well and soak them, except the liver, in salted water for ½ to 1 hour before cooking. They are generally used to make stock for gravy or soup or for giblet pie.

How to Stuff Poultry

1. Fill the neck end with stuffing until the breast is plump, then draw the skin backwards over the neck and sew or skewer firmly. If sewn use a coarse needle and thick white cotton.
2. Fill the body from the other end with the stuffing and push the tail through the slit and skewer firmly.

How to Truss Poultry

Draw the thighs close to the body and cross the legs over the tail. Tie firmly with string. Fold the wings backwards and inwards over the neck skin, tie or skewer into position.

How to Prepare Hares and Rabbits for Cooking

HOW TO SKIN
1. Cut off all legs at the first joints.
2. Slit the skin all along the belly and loosen it from the body, draw it over the hind legs.
3. Then pull the skin towards the head and off the forelegs.

HOW TO CLEAN. Slit the belly and draw out the insides, keeping the heart and liver for stuffing or stock. Wash the rabbit well in cold water.

TO TRUSS. Skewer or tie the legs close to the body.

TO JOINT. Cut off the hind legs close to the body. Remove head. Cut the body into 3 or 4 pieces through the backbone. Cut the piece with forelegs attached in half lengthwise. Remove eyes, split head in half lengthwise and use it for stock.

How to Boil Unsalted or Fresh Meat, Game and Poultry

1. Use a pan just large enough to hold the meat, with water to cover. The less liquid the better will be the flavour.
2. Bring the water to the boil; add a bouquet garni (see page 11) and an onion stuck with 3 or 4 cloves.
3. Put meat into boiling water and boil rapidly for 5 minutes. Skim well and put on the lid.
4. Reduce the heat and simmer gently until the meat is tender (see below). Test with a fine skewer which should go in easily if the meat is tender.
5. If desired, root vegetables cut in large pieces may be cooked with the meat and served as a garnish. Add salt (1 level tablespoon) with the vegetables.
6. Use the liquid for soups, sauces and gravy.

How to Boil Salted Meat

1. If the meat is known to be very salty soak it in cold water 3–4 hours or longer.
2. Place the meat in a pan with just enough cold water to cover.
3. Bring the water slowly to the boil and add an onion stuck with 5 or 6 cloves, 5 or 6 peppercorns and a bay leaf.
4. Skim, cover the pan and simmer for the required time.
5. If the meat is to be served hot, potatoes, carrots and other vegetables may be cooked with it.
6. If the meat is to be served cold, leave it to cool in the liquor.
7. If the liquor is not too salty it will make an excellent soup or stock for lentil, bean or vegetable soup.

Boiling Time-table for Meat, Game and Poultry

Beef, fresh	20 minutes per lb. and 20 minutes over.
Brains, calf's	20 minutes or 10 minutes if to be fried afterwards.
Brains, ox	30 minutes.
Brains, sheep's and pig's	15 minutes.
Ears, pig's	1½ hours.
Feet, calf's and cow's	2–3 hours.
Feet, pigs	2 hours.
Fowl	1–2½ hours according to age of bird and size.
Head, calf's	3–4 hours.
Head, pig's cheek	1½–2 hours.
Head, sheep's	1½–2 hours.
Mutton	15–20 minutes per lb.
Pork	25–30 minutes per lb.
Rabbit	40–60 minutes.
Salted meat	25–30 minutes per lb, plus 25–30 minutes.
Tongue, calf's	Cooked with the head.
Tongue, ox	3–3½ hours.
Tongue, sheep's and pig's	1½–2 hours.
Veal	20–25 minutes per lb.

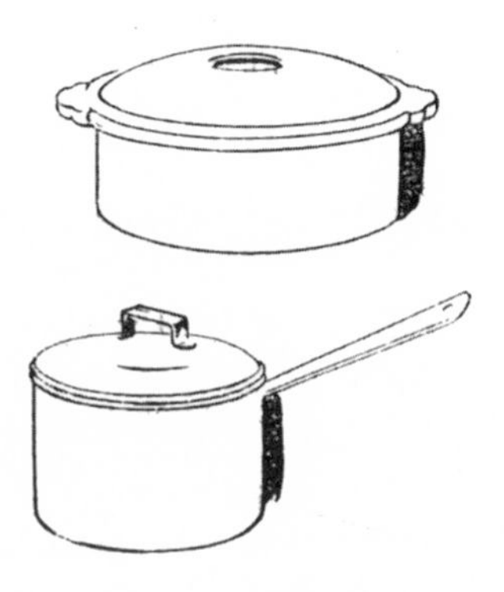

How to Stew

Whatever recipe is being used, the following rules must be followed:

1. Never let a stew boil. Only an occasional bubble should show on the surface of the liquid.
2. Be careful not to add too much liquid. A stew should be thick. If vegetables are used with the meat less liquid is needed as some water comes out of the vegetables.

3. Use onions or leeks, mixed vegetables, herbs and spices to give an interesting flavour.
4. If root vegetables are old, cut them in very small pieces before adding or they may not cook sufficiently.
5. Stews may be cooked on the top of the stove in a saucepan with a tightly fitting lid or in a covered dish or casserole in the oven. Time 1½–3 hours.

Roasting

The following three methods of roasting are those most commonly used. The choice of the method depends on the kind of meat being cooked (see "Cuts of Meat and Their Use", pages 35–39), on the other foods which are to be cooked in the oven at the same time, and on personal preference.

An uncovered roasting pan is recommended.

Method 1. The meat is browned or "seared" at a very high temperature for a short time and the cooking finished at a lower temperature.
1. Place the meat in the roasting pan: if the joint is lean, add some extra fat or dripping.
2. Place it in a very hot oven (500° F.) for 15–20 minutes or until the meat is brown.
3. Reduce the heat to slow or moderate (about 350° F.) and continue cooking. (For times see page 36.)

N.B. — This process may be reversed, that is, cook the meat at 350° F. and then raise the temperature to 500° F. for the last 15–20 minutes. This method is useful if there are potatoes to brown or Yorkshire pudding to cook at the end.

Method 2. The meat is cooked all the time at a moderate temperature. This method is better suited to large joints, as small joints are not in the oven long enough to become well browned. Proceed as in Method 1 but place the meat in a moderate oven (375° F.–400° F.) and keep it at the same temperature all the time.

Method 3. Slow roasting, when the meat is cooked as in Method 2, but at a lower temperature, 325° F.–350° F. Meat cooked this way takes longer than the other methods but it is an excellent way of roasting the cheaper cuts. (See pages 35–38.)

Basting

(See page 10)

Basting is not necessary with a reasonably fatty joint, especially if the fat side is uppermost. Lean joints are improved by basting and so is the crackling of pork. Poultry, game and offal need basting every 15–30 minutes, or, alternatively, strips of fat bacon may be laid across the top.

Frozen Meat

This should be allowed to thaw before roasting, but to avoid excessive loss of juice, cook it as soon as possible after thawing. If it has to go in the oven before it has completely thawed allow slightly longer cooking times and use Method 3, otherwise the inside will be raw and the outside over-cooked.

Roasting Time-table

The following times are intended as a guide. The time needed depends on the shape and thickness of the joint as well as the weight. The joints which take longest are the boned and rolled ribs of beef and any meat which has been boned and stuffed. Lamb, veal and pork should always be well done, but beef may be cooked well or underdone according to personal preference. The times given below are for well-done meat, and for joints weighing 3–8 lb. Larger joints need less time per lb., smaller joints longer.

Meat	*Methods 1 and 2*		*Method 3*
Beef or Mutton	Thick cut	30 mins. per lb.	40 mins. per lb.
	Thin cut	25 mins. per lb.	30 mins. per lb.
Lamb		30 mins. per lb.	40 mins. per lb.
Pork	Thick cuts	35 mins. per lb.	45 mins. per lb.
	Thin cuts	30 mins. per lb.	40 mins. per lb.
Veal		30–40 mins. per lb.	40–50 mins. per lb.
Chicken, Rabbit and Duck		50 mins.–1 hour	2 hours
Duckling		35 mins.	
Goose or young Hare		1½ hours–2 hours	2 hours
Turkey Drawn weight,	7–10 lb.	2 hours	3 hours
	10–12 lb.	3 hours	4 hours
	15–20 lb.	3½ hours	4½ hours
Heart, sheep's	–	–	1½ hours
Heart, ox	–	–	3–4 hours
Heart, calf's	–	–	2 hours

Pot Roasting

This is cooking meat in a little fat in a saucepan with the lid on. It is useful if no oven is available, but a thick heavy saucepan is *essential.*

1. Melt enough fat to cover the bottom of the saucepan.
2. When the fat is hot, add the joint and brown well on all sides.
3. Put the lid on (which must fit tightly), reduce the heat and cook slowly. Allow the same time as for slow roasting. (See Method 3 on page 42.) If the joint is lean, baste occasionally.

Braising

This is a combination of pot roasting and stewing and is very good for cheaper cuts of meat. If fat joints are used it is wiser to remove surplus fat before cooking or the vegetables and gravy will be greasy.

1. Brown the meat as in "Pot Roasting", then remove it from the saucepan and pour off any surplus fat.
2. Place in the saucepan a thick layer of root vegetables cut in pieces, add a bouquet garni, season with salt.

3. Add about 1 in. of stock or water, place the meat on top of the vegetables, place the lid on the pan and simmer gently until the meat is tender. Allow the same time as for "Slow Roasting", Method 3, page 42. Braising may be done in a casserole in the oven.
4. Serve the meat garnished with the vegetables and serve the gravy separately.

How to Fry Meat

(See "Fats and Oil", page 58.)

How to Grill Meat

(See "Grilling", page 13.)

Carving

On page 35 is a picture of the bundles of fibres of which meat is composed. For carving it is essential to cut *across* these fibres. This makes the meat easier to bite than if it is carved *with* the fibres, and the meat appears to be more tender.

The next essential is to have a really sharp carving knife. Cut meat as thinly as possible. It is more pleasant to eat than thick slices. Some people prefer to carve lamb, mutton and pork thicker than beef.

The following diagrams show how to carve joints which beginners often find difficult:

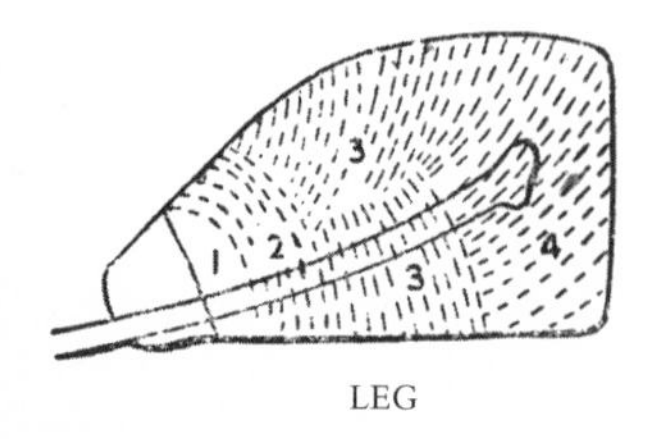

LEG

LEG OF LAMB, MUTTON OR PORK

Make a cut straight down to the bone at (1). Then cut slightly slanting slices at (2), then (3) and finish at (4). Be careful that the slices are always across the grain of the meat.

BRISKET

BRISKET OF BEEF
Cut slices downwards along the dotted lines (1) to (2) and cut down close to the bone.

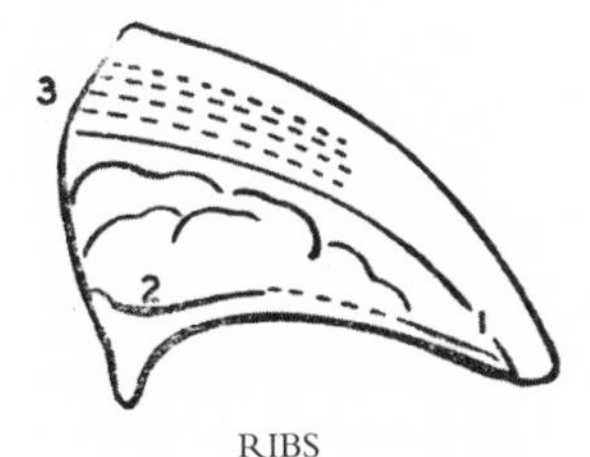

RIBS

RIBS OF BEEF
Run the knife along the bone from (1) to (2) to loosen the meat. Then slice downwards along the dotted lines (3).

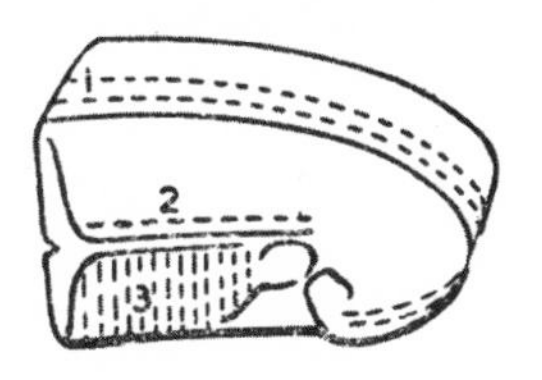

SIRLOIN

BEEF SIRLOIN
Cut downwards along the dotted line (1) and then loosen the slices from the bone at (2). Cut the lower part along the dotted lines (3).

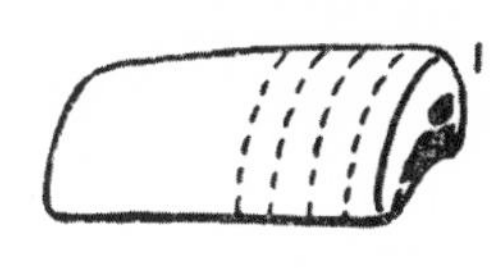

LOIN

LOIN OR NECK
Cut down along the dotted lines, cutting off one chop at a time. The bones should be jointed before cooking.

CALF'S HEAD

CALF'S HEAD
Cut through to the bone along the dotted lines (1) and (2). Serve some meat from each part of the head and a slice of the tongue.

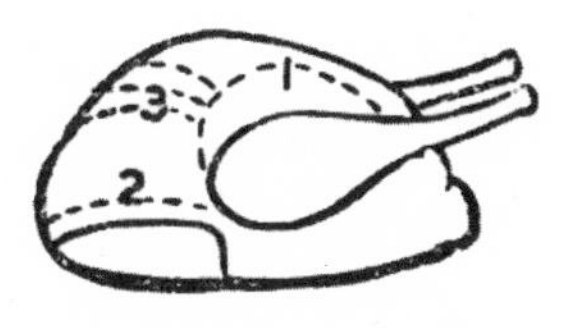

CHICKEN

POULTRY
Remove the legs by cutting through the skin at (1) and, pressing outwards with the knife, pull off the leg. Do the same with the wing, cutting at (2). Then cut slices of the breast meat, cutting downwards at (3).

What to Serve with Meat, Game and Poultry

The following tables give some suggestions for vegetables, sauces and accompaniments for meat, game and poultry. The use of different accompaniments gives variety to the menu as well as improving the general flavour and texture of the dish. Some of these suggestions are traditional English customs, others are from the menus of European countries, the U.S.A. and the Dominions.

BEEF

Roast Beef

Potatoes	Roast or boiled
Other Vegetables	Any green vegetable, carrots, peas, green beans, parsnips, marrow or pumpkin.
Sauces and Accompaniments	Brown gravy. Horseradish sauce. Yorkshire pudding.

Grilled Steak

Potatoes	Fried or boiled
Other Vegetables	Fried onions or mushrooms, beetroot, watercress, lettuce, grilled or baked tomatoes.
Sauces and Accompaniments	Parsley butter. Tart jelly (currant, cranberry, sloe, etc.). Grated horseradish.

Boiled Beef

Potatoes	Boiled
Other Vegetables	Onions, tomatoes, turnips, carrots, beetroot.
Sauces and Accompaniments	Dumplings.

Stewed Beef

Potatoes	Boiled
Other Vegetables	Any root vegetables.
Sauces and Accompaniments	Dumplings.

Braised Beef

Potatoes	Mashed, boiled or baked
Other Vegetables	Peas, green beans, carrots, turnips, celery, and any green vegetable.
Sauces and Accompaniments	Horseradish sauce. Tart jelly. Gravy.

Minced Beef or Hamburger

Potatoes	Boiled, mashed or fried
Other Vegetables	Carrots, tomatoes, peas, onions and any green vegetable.
Sauces and Accompaniments	Tart jelly. Pickles. Tomato sauce. Gravy.

Cold Beef

Potatoes	Boiled or potato salad
Other Vegetables	Beetroot. Green salad.
Sauces and Accompaniments	Tart jelly. Pickles, including cabbage or cucumber.

LAMB OR MUTTON

Roast Mutton

Potatoes	Roast or boiled
Other Vegetables	Peas, turnips, swedes, any green vegetable.
Sauces and Accompaniments	Savoury stuffing. Currant jelly. Brown gravy. Onion sauce.

Roast Lamb

Potatoes	Roast or boiled
Other Vegetables	Peas, turnips, swedes, any green vegetable.
Sauces and Accompaniments	Mint sauce.

Grilled or Fried Chops

Potatoes	Mashed or fried
Other Vegetables	Spinach, peas, green beans, tomatoes, mushrooms.

Sauces and Accompaniments	Mint sauce. Mint or currant jelly. Tomato or mushroom sauce. Parsley butter.
Boiled Leg	
Potatoes	Boiled jacket
Other Vegetables	Swedes, carrots, turnips, and any green vegetable.
Sauces and Accompaniments	Caper sauce. Red currant jelly. Parsley sauce. Onion sauce. Fennel sauce.
Stewed	
Potatoes	Boiled jacket
Other Vegetables	Carrots, swedes, celery, peas, green beans, turnips.
Sauces and Accompaniments	Pickled red cabbage. Dumplings.
Braised	
Potatoes	Boiled, mashed or baked jacket
Other Vegetables	Swedes, turnips, onions, carrots, any green vegetable.
Sauces and Accompaniments	Mint sauce. Tart jelly. Pickled cucumber.

PORK

Roast	
Potatoes	Boiled or roast or mashed
Other Vegetables	Cauliflower, onions, cabbage, celery, tomatoes, spinach, sprouts.
Sauces and Accompaniments	Sage and onion stuffing. Brown gravy. Baked or fried apples or apple sauce. Tart jelly. Cranberry sauce.
Grilled or Fried Chops	
Potatoes	Mashed or fried
Other Vegetables	Onions, carrots, celery, tomatoes, turnips.
Sauces and Accompaniments	Fried apple rings. Tart jelly.
Boiled Salt Pork	
Potatoes	Boiled
Other Vegetables	Cabbage, pease pudding.
Sauces and Accompaniments	Tomato sauce. Dumplings.
Grilled or Fried Gammon	
Potatoes	Mashed or fried
Other Vegetables	Spinach, peas, tomatoes.
Sauces and Accompaniments	Apple sauce or fried apple.
Boiled Bacon	
Potatoes	Boiled
Other Vegetables	Cabbage, carrots, beetroot, turnips.
Sauces and Accompaniments	Pease pudding. Beans. Parsley sauce.
Sausages	
Potatoes	Mashed or fried
Other Vegetables	Any green vegetable, tomatoes.
Sauces and Accompaniments	Fried apple rings or apple sauce. Fried bacon. Gravy. Fried onions.

VEAL

Roast	
Potatoes	Boiled, roast or mashed
Other Vegetables	Spinach, tomatoes, onions, beetroot.
Sauces and Accompaniments	Savoury stuffing. Brown gravy. Boiled bacon or salt pork.
Grilled or Fried Chops and Cutlets	
Potatoes	Mashed or fried
Other Vegetables	Tomatoes, carrots, celery, string beans.
Sauces and Accompaniments	Tomato sauce. Apple sauce or fried apples. Celery sauce. Lemon.

Calf's Head	
Potatoes	Boiled
Other Vegetables	Green salad to follow.
Sauces and Accompaniments	Vinaigrette sauce with the brains.
Liver	
Potatoes	Fried, baked, jacket, boiled or mashed
Other Vegetables	Spinach, tomatoes, green salad.
Sauces and Accompaniments	Bacon. Brown gravy. Savoury forcemeat.

POULTRY AND GAME

Roast Chicken	
Potatoes	Mashed, fried or roast
Other Vegetables	Onions, cauliflower, peas, roast green beans, celery, watercress, green salad.
Sauces and Accompaniments	Savoury stuffing. Currant jelly. Bread sauce. Brown gravy. Bacon rolls.
Boiled Rabbit	
Potatoes	Boiled jacket
Other Vegetables	Onions, carrots, turnips, and any green vegetable.
Sauces and Accompaniments	Boiled salt pork or bacon. Dumplings. Parsley sauce. Mint sauce.
Roast Duck	
Potatoes	Boiled or roast
Other Vegetables	Peas, carrots, turnips, and any green vegetable, orange salad.
Sauces and Accompaniments	Apple sauce. Sage and onion stuffing. Tart jelly.
Roast Turkey	
Potatoes	Boiled, fried or roast
Other Vegetables	Onions, peas, pumpkin, sprouts.
Sauces and Accompaniments	Sausages. Cranberry sauce. Brown gravy. Chestnut stuffing. Bacon rolls. Bread sauce. Celery sauce.
Roast Goose	
Potatoes	Roast or boiled
Other Vegetables	Onions, carrots and any green vegetable.
Sauces and Accompaniments	Sage and onion stuffing. Apple and prune stuffing. Apple sauce. Brown gravy. Savoury stuffing. Currant jelly. Cranberry sauce.
Stewed or Jugged Hare	
Potatoes	Boiled, jacket or mashed
Other Vegetables	Any green vegetable.
Sauces and Accompaniments	Currant jelly. Forcemeat balls.
Roast Rabbit or Hare	
Potatoes	Roast, baked, jacket or boiled
Other Vegetables	Any green vegetable, onions, carrots.
Sauces and Accompaniments	Red currant jelly. Brown gravy. Savoury stuffing.
Boiled Chicken	
Potatoes	Boiled
Other Vegetables	Any green or root vegetables.
Sauces and Accompaniments	Onion sauce. Bread sauce. Egg sauce. Parsley sauce.

USING UP COOKED MEAT. Meat which has been cooked should be re-heated very gently, preferably below boiling point. It needs plenty of seasoning. The best way of reheating a joint is to cut the meat in very thin slices and pour over well seasoned boiling gravy or sauce. No further heating will be needed.

10 *Vegetables and Salads*

Vegetables may be divided into four main classes:

1. Green leafy vegetables such as the cabbage family, spinach, kale, watercress and lettuce.
2. Roots and tubers such as potatoes, carrots, turnips, swedes, beetroot, parsnips, and Jerusalem artichokes.
3. Legumes or pulses such as fresh or dried peas, beans, lentils and split peas.
4. Other vegetables such as pumpkin, marrow, asparagus and the onion family (onions, leeks, chives and shallots).

Storing Vegetables

(See page 8.)

Ways of Cooking and Serving Vegetables

GROUP 1 — GREEN LEAFY VEGETABLES

The best method of cooking is in a little hot fat (see page 50) or in a very little boiling salted water (see below). They may then be served as an accompaniment to meat, fish, egg or cheese dishes, or combined with sauces in savoury dishes such as "Vegetable au gratin". One of the best ways of serving all these vegetables is raw in salads (see page 53).

GROUP 2 — ROOTS AND TUBERS

These may be cooked in fat (see page 51), boiled (see below), baked (see page 52) or fried (see page 51). Serve in the same way as vegetables in Group 1.

GROUP 3 — LEGUMES OR PULSES

When fresh they may be cooked and served in any of the ways described for Groups 1 and 2.

When dried they should be boiled (see page 51). Cooked legumes are also used in salads. Legumes combined with eggs, cheese or milk make good meat substitutes.

GROUP 4

These vegetables may be cooked by any of the methods described for Groups 1 and 2.

How to Boil Green and Root Vegetables (Except Potatoes)

If vegetables are cooked carelessly much of their food value is lost. Their Vitamin C – the fresh fruit vitamin – is easily destroyed by bad cooking. Throwing away the cooking water also wastes valuable mineral salts and vitamins.

So when you cook vegetables follow these rules:

1. Use as fresh as possible. If you grow your own vegetables do not gather them until you need them.

2. Wash the vegetables thoroughly, but avoid soaking where possible and never soak for long. Half an hour in cold water is enough for even the most tight-hearted cabbage.

3. Scrub root vegetables and scrape them, or if tough-skinned peel off the outer layer. Remove the dark outer leaves of cabbage and use these shredded in soups or stews. Do not throw them away because they contain more of the vitamins and mineral salts than the more tender inner leaves.

4. Slice root vegetables and shred the green ones. Break cauliflower into sprigs. They cook more quickly this way.

5. Never drown vegetables. You need only just enough water to keep the pan from burning. Usually ¼ pint will do. As less water is used less salt is needed, 1 level teaspoon to 1 lb. of vegetables.

6. Cook with the lid on the pan. If no lid is available a plate can be used. This point is important because the vegetables are to be "steam boiled" and if the steam is allowed to escape the pan will go dry and burn.

7. Boil for 10–15 minutes, giving the pan an occasional shake. Old root vegetables may require longer.

8. Drain off any liquid and use for making soups and gravies or thicken with flour (1 oz. to ½ pint) and use as a sauce (see page 65).

9. Serve the vegetables at once. Keeping hot or reheating will destroy the Vitamin C. Before serving, if you can spare a teaspoonful of margarine, add it to the vegetables and toss well.

How to Cook Vegetables in Fat

1. Prepare the vegetables as described for boiling.

2. Heat sufficient lard, cooking fat, dripping or oil to cover the bottom of the saucepan. A mixture of these fats may be used.

3. When the fat is hot, but not smoking, add the vegetables and seasoning and cover with a tightly fitting lid.

4. Cook over a moderate heat until tender, 10–20 minutes according to the vegetable.

5. Serve at once with any liquid there may be in the pan.

How to Boil Dried Peas, Beans, Lentils and Split Peas

1. Cover with boiling water and soak overnight. If peas or beans are very old and hard add bicarbonate of soda to the soaking water (1 level teaspoon soda to 1 lb. peas or beans).
2. Cook in the water in which they have been soaked. Bring to the boil and boil gently until tender (1–2 hours). The time depends on the variety being cooked. Cook with the lid on the pan.
3. For extra flavour add a sprig of mint or a pinch of dried mint to peas. Add an onion or leek, a carrot and bouquet garni (or some bacon rinds and a few cloves) to beans, lentils or split peas.
4. Use the cooking liquid for soup, stock or gravy, and sauces.

How to Boil Potatoes

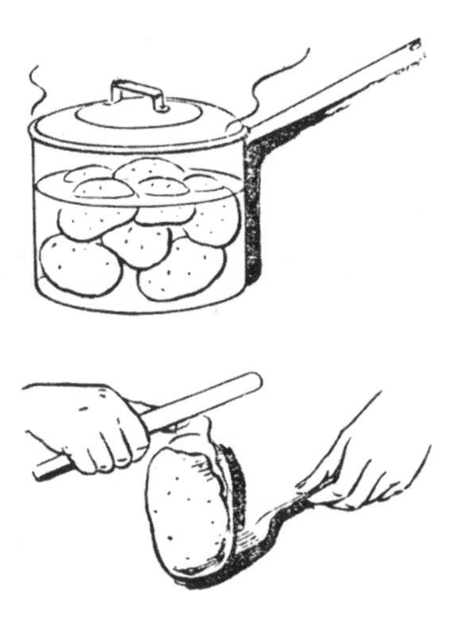

1. Choose potatoes of the same size; cut large ones. Scrub well.
2. Put into boiling salted water using just enough water to cover. (1 level tablespoon of salt to 1 lb. of potatoes.)
3. Cook with the lid on until tender (15–20 minutes).
4. Drain carefully.
5. Shake gently in pan over low heat for a minute or two to dry them and leave them deliciously floury.
6. If mashed potatoes are required, peel as soon as they are cooked.

Steaming Vegetables

Although it is often convenient to steam vegetables when using a steamer to cook a complete meal, the method is not recommended. Boiling is preferable to steaming as there is less loss of Vitamin C. If vegetables are steamed a raw vegetable salad should be served with the meal to compensate for loss of Vitamin C, or, alternatively, sprinkle the vegetables with freshly chopped parsley just before serving.

How to Fry Vegetables

Potatoes are the vegetables most commonly fried, either raw or cooked. Other cooked root vegetables are often fried in shallow fat or made into croquettes and fried in deep fat.

For details of frying, see "Fats and Oils", page 58.

How to Bake Vegetables

(This includes any vegetables cooked in the oven.)

Green leafy vegetables (see page 49) are not suitable for cooking in the oven.

The following are the baking methods most commonly used:
1. **In their jackets, that is, without peeling**. Suitable for potatoes, beetroot and onions. The vegetables are washed and placed on the oven shelf or on a baking tray.

POTATOES. Prick the skin before baking to prevent the potatoes from bursting. Bake in a moderate oven for 45 minutes or until cooked. Test by squeezing the potato in a cloth and if soft it is cooked. Prick the skin again to allow the steam to escape and make the inside floury. Baked potatoes may have the insides removed, mashed and seasoned and returned to the potato shell for reheating. These are called stuffed potatoes. Cooked meat or fish or grated cheese and cooked vegetables may be mixed with the mashed potato to form a savoury stuffing.

BEETROOT. Bake in a slow or moderate oven until tender. Test by pinching the skin and if it comes off easily the beetroot is cooked.
Time — 1–2 hours, depending on the size.

ONIONS. Bake in a moderate oven until soft when squeezed.
Time — 40 minutes to 1 hour, depending on the size.

2. **In a covered dish or casserole**. Suitable for all except the green leafy vegetables. Slice or dice the vegetables and place in the dish with a little fat, salt and sufficient water to moisten the bottom. Cover and bake in a moderate oven until tender. Time — 30 minutes to 1 hour.
3. **Baked or roasted in hot fat either round the joint or in a separate pan**. Suitable for potatoes, carrots, parsnips, marrow pumpkin, turnip, onions and swedes. Peel and cut the vegetables in pieces, or, if small, leave whole. Bake in a moderately hot oven until tender.
Time — 40 minutes to 1 hour.
4. **Sliced thinly, covered with milk and baked in a pie dish in a moderate oven**. The top is usually sprinkled thickly with browned bread crumbs. Suitable for all root vegetables.
Time — 1 to 2 hours.

Salads

Suitable Vegetables for Salads

GREEN LEAF VEGETABLES. At least one of these should be included in every salad: raw cabbage heart, savoy, spinach, sprouts, young leaves of kale and young turnip tops, watercress including the stalks, parsley, young dandelion leaves, mint, nasturtium leaves, young celery leaves, green tops of leeks or spring onions, chives, mustard and cress, all green herbs, lettuce or endive.

ROOT VEGETABLES. Raw or cooked beetroot, turnip, parsnip, carrot, kohl rabi, swede, cooked potato.

OTHER VEGETABLES. Raw radishes, cucumber, onions, leeks, cooked or raw peas, cooked French or runner beans, celery, chicory, cauliflower and broccoli, cooked broad beans.

Tips for the Salad Maker

1. When making salads touch the leaves as little as possible. Use directly after picking or buying. If this is not convenient a saucepan with a well-fitting lid placed on a cool floor is excellent for keeping salad vegetables crisp.
2. Just before serving, wash leaves carefully, shake off the water gently and shake dry in a clean cloth or in a wire salad basket if you have one. Outside leaves should be saved for soup.
3. Shred raw green vegetables with a sharp knife. Parsley should be coarsely chopped.
4. Root vegetables such as carrots should be washed and scraped lightly, then shredded or grated. Alternatively, they may be cooked and chopped or sliced when cold. Potatoes should be used cooked and cold. The thick skins of turnips and swedes should be removed by peeling.
5. Be sure the salad is well flavoured. Use green herbs, chives, spring onions, celery, nasturtium leaves and salad dressing.
6. Add colour to the salad by using raw grated carrot, beetroot, swede, whole or sliced tomato, radishes or hard boiled eggs.
7. Serve as soon as possible after preparation.
8. If a salad is served as a main dish or as the only green vegetable, provide at least 3 oz. (i.e., one to two breakfastcups) of raw vegetables per person. At least half of this should be green vegetables.

Salad Dressing

FRENCH DRESSING. This is the simplest dressing consisting of oil, vinegar and seasoning, and the most suitable for green salads. Turn the salad over and over in the dressing to coat it well. Serve the salad as soon as it has been dressed.

BOILED SALAD DRESSINGS. These have a plain sauce base (see page 65) with added vinegar, eggs and seasoning. They are good for meat, fish, egg and fruit salads and are less rich than mayonnaise which contains a great deal of oil.

MAYONNAISE. This is used chiefly with egg, meat and fish salads. It has a foundation of egg yolk, vinegar and seasoning with a large amount of oil. The vinegar should be mixed with the egg yolk before any oil is added or there may be difficulty in making the oil and egg mix. All ingredients should be kept at the same temperature (cool), and the oil should be beaten into the egg and vinegar literally drop by drop.

11 *Fruit*

Fruit may be divided into three classes:

1. Fresh fruit which is served raw, stewed, baked or in pies and puddings.
2. Dried fruit which is served uncooked, stewed, or in cakes and puddings.
3. Canned or bottled fruit which may be used in puddings and pies but is best served without cooking.

How to Prepare Fruit

APPLES. Wash, core and remove the stalks and any bruised parts. For baking leave the skins on but remove the cores. For stewing peel and leave whole, or core and cut in quarters. For puddings and pies, peel, core and slice. For purée the apples merely need to be washed and cut in sections.

If peeled apples are not to be cooked at once put them into cold salted water to prevent them from turning brown (use 1 level tablespoon salt to 1 quart of water).

DRIED APPLES. (See "Dried Fruit".)

APRICOTS. Wash and dry well. If for fruit salad cut in half and remove the stones.

DRIED APRICOTS. (See "Dried Fruit".)

BANANAS. Peel. If required for fruit salad do not slice until the salad is to be mixed, as they quickly turn brown.

BLACKBERRIES. Pick over and remove stalks, hulls and any damaged fruit. If dirty wash and drain thoroughly. Examine for grubs. If the blackberries are not to be used at once spread them in a shallow dish as they keep better this way. If left in a heap in a basket or basin they very quickly become mouldy.

CHERRIES. Wash well. Leave the stalks on if the cherries are to be served for dessert; for fruit salad remove the stalks and stones; for pies, stewing, etc., remove the stalks.

CRANBERRIES. Pick over the discarded stalks, leaves and any damaged fruit. Wash and drain well.

CURRANTS (black, white and red). Wash the bunches well. To remove the fruit from the stalks, use a fork for stripping off the berries. Do not stalk them until they are to be used as they keep better on the stalks. Spread in a shallow dish for keeping (see "Blackberries").

DRIED CURRANTS. (See "Dried Fruit".)

DAMSONS. Wash well and remove stalks, leaves and any damaged fruit.

DRIED FRUIT.
1. Apples, pears, prunes, apricots and figs. Wash well and soak overnight in water to cover if the fruit is old and hard. The time required for soaking depends on the condition of the fruit. Some fruit may be cooked without any soaking.
2. Currants, sultanas, raisins and dates. If dirty wash well but make sure they are thoroughly dry before use.

ELDERBERRIES. (See "Currants".)

FIGS. Raw. Wash well and serve whole or sliced. For stewing, wash well and remove stalks.

Dried. (See "Dried Fruit".)

GOOSEBERRIES. Wash well and remove tops and tails. Kitchen scissors are the quickest for this job.

GRAPES. Wash and drain well. If required for fruit salads, remove the seeds.

GRAPEFRUIT. If for fruit salads peel and remove all white pith and the pips. If to be served in their skins cut each grapefruit in half. Remove the seeds with a fork and with a sharp pointed vegetable knife cut along each side of the membrane between the sections of fruit, loosening the flesh from the membrane. Then loosen the membrane at the outer edges and under the core. Lift up the core and the membrane should come with it, leaving behind the flesh.

GREENGAGES. Wash well and remove the stalks. If to be served in fruit salad remove the stones.

LEMONS. Wash well. If the rind is to be used grated, do this before squeezing out the juice as it is difficult to grate afterwards. Use a medium sized grater, not the nutmeg size, and grate only the yellow part as the white pith is bitter.

To squeeze out the juice easily first roll the lemon on a board with the hand for a minute or two, pressing hard and then cut and squeeze out the juice.

To use sections for garnishing, cut in slices, quarters or fancy shapes.

LOGANBERRIES. As for Blackberries.

NECTARINES. Wash and dry carefully. For fruit salad or pies remove the stones and slice.

ORANGES. For using rind and juice, see "Lemons". For serving in the skin, see "Grapefruit".

PEACHES. Wash and dry carefully. For fruit salad or pies remove the stones and if the skins are thick and rough they should be removed by blanching for 1–2 minutes (see page 10).

PEARS. For stewing, wash, peel and cook whole or in halves or quarters. For baking, wash and peel or leave the skins on. When peeled and not required immediately for cooking put in salted water (see "Apples").

PLUMS. (See "Greengages".)

QUINCES. Wash, peel and core and cut in thin slices.

RASPBERRIES. As for Blackberries.

RHUBARB. Wash well and trim the ends. Do not remove the skin unless the rhubarb is very old and stringy. It is a better colour with the skin left on.

STRAWBERRIES. (See "Blackberries".)

How to Serve Fruit Raw

For the preparation of fruit, see above.

Fruit such as berries and currants should be sprinkled with sugar and left to stand half an hour before serving.

Grapefruit halves should be sprinkled with ½–1 level tablespoon of sugar and left to stand 10–20 minutes before serving.

Other fruit is generally served whole. Quinces, rhubarb, green gooseberries, green apples and cooking pears are not suitable for serving raw.

Fresh Fruit Salad

1. Make a syrup by boiling together 2–4 oz. of sugar and ½ pint of water. When the sugar has dissolved remove from the heat and cool.
2. Prepare the fruit (see pages 42–44) and cut it in small even sized pieces as this gives the best blend of flavours.
3. Put the fruit in the serving dish and pour over sufficient syrup to moisten well. Serve very cold.

How to Stew Fresh Fruit

1. Make a syrup by heating sugar and water together until the sugar dissolves. The amount of sugar depends on the tartness of the fruit and whether you have

a sweet tooth. 4 oz. of sugar is an average amount for 1 lb. of tart fruit and ½ pint of water should be sufficient liquid.

2. When the sugar is dissolved add the fruit and cook it very gently until it is just tender. The fruit keeps its appearance better if the liquid is kept just below boiling point, that is, simmering. Turn the fruit over in the syrup once or twice. Keep the lid on the pan for apples and pears.

3. When it is tender but not pulped, drain from the syrup and place in a serving dish. The time varies with the kind of fruit and the degree of ripeness, but the following is a guide:

Berries, currants and other small fruit	15–20 minutes.
Quartered apples, plums, etc.	20–30 minutes.
Cooking pears	½–1 hour (may be 2–3 hours for very hard kinds).
Quinces	1½–2 hours.

4. Boil the syrup rapidly to drive off some of the water and make it thick. Then pour the syrup over the fruit and serve hot or cold.

Flavourings may be added to the syrup. Use lemon and orange peel, cloves, spices, ginger, etc. When sugar is short, stew the fruit in water and add sugar at the end. Less sugar will be needed.

How to Stew Dried Fruit

Proceed as above except that the soaking water is used for cooking. Less sugar is needed with dried fruit and it may be boiled as it is less likely to lose its appearance than fresh fruit. The times depend on the age of the fruit, the length of time it has been soaked, and the method used for drying. Approximate times are ½ to 1 hour.

Stewing Fruit in the Oven

This is an excellent way of cooking all kinds of fruit. Any dish with a well-fitting lid is suitable.

1. Prepare the fruit as for stewing (see pages 54–56).

2. Add the sugar and only enough water to moisten the dish, or with fruits which are very juicy such as berries, rhubarb and ripe plums no water need be added; quinces and hard pears will need ½ pint to 1 lb. of fruit.

3. Cover and cook in a slow to moderate oven until tender. The times are the same as for stewing (see above).

How to Bake Apples and Pears

1. Prepare the fruit (see pages 54–56). If the apples have not been cored, slit the skin with a sharp knife, making a ring near the top. This will prevent the skin from bursting during cooking.

2. Cored apples may be stuffed with chopped dried fruit. Place the apples or pears in a shallow baking dish (without a lid). Add sugar or syrup, 1–2 tablespoons for each apple or pear and about ¼ in. of water.
3. Bake in a moderate oven until the fruit is tender, basting (see page 10) occasionally with the liquid. The time depends on the kind of fruit; 40–50 minutes for apples and 45–60 minutes for pears, although very hard cooking pears may take longer. Serve hot or cold.

How to Make a Fruit Purée or Pulp

This is merely stewed fruit rubbed through a sieve to make a fine smooth pulp. It is used for fruit fools, whips, jellies, sauces and other similar dishes. If a thick pulp is required do not use the juice, or better still, cook the fruit with little if any added liquid. The oven method is the best for this, and gives a much better flavoured pulp.

How to Make Fruit Pies, Puddings and Tarts

(See "Batters, Cakes and Pastry", page 73.)

12 *Fats, Oils and Frying*

FATS are solid at ordinary room temperatures and melt when heated. Those used in cooking are butter, margarine, lard, suet, cooking fats and clarified dripping (see pages 60–61). Peanut butter is a fat used in dishes where the flavour of peanuts is not a disadvantage.

OILS are liquid at ordinary room temperatures but may thicken in very cold weather. They are generally used for frying or for salad dressings and mayonnaise but may be used for making pastry. Olive oil and vegetable and nut oils are the most common. Cod liver oil and halibut liver oil contain Vitamins A and D and are used as supplements to the diet for babies, small children, expectant and nursing mothers.

STORAGE. Fats and oils absorb flavours very readily and should be stored away from foods which have a strong odour. This property of fats is made use of in certain cooking methods, for example, essences combine better in cake mixtures if they are added to the creamed fat; and a little fat in a fruit pie improves the flavour.

Fats Suitable for Pastry, Cakes and Puddings

The two most important points in the selection of a fat for pastry, cakes and puddings are the flavour and what is known as the "shortening power" of the fat. A fat which has a high shortening power makes a more tender cake and a shorter pastry than other fats. It creams more readily and makes a finer and lighter cake or pudding mixture. Fats with a high shortening power are lard, most cooking fats and beef dripping. These will make the shortest pastry. In cake making it is better to use half margarine or butter and half lard, cooking fat or beef dripping, as the last three fats sometimes have a pronounced flavour. For cakes where no essence or flavouring is added it is better to use all margarine or butter.

Fats Suitable for Frying

A good frying fat should be free from moisture which makes it splutter when heated, and it should have what is known as a high "smoking temperature". When fat is heated it first of all melts, and then bubbles if there is any moisture in it. The bubbling is caused by the water being turned to steam and forced out of the fat. When it has finished bubbling the surface is still and presently a faint blue haze rises from the surface. If the fat is heated beyond this temperature it smokes and burns and is spoilt for further frying. A good frying fat is one which can be heated to a high temperature (not less than 360° F.) before it smokes and burns, that is, it has a high smoking temperature. This is important because the fat must be hot enough to form a coating quickly on the outside of the food. This coating protects the food inside from becoming greasy.

Vegetable oils generally have a high smoking temperature and this is why they are commonly used for frying. A mixture of half beef and half mutton dripping also makes a good frying fat. Margarine and butter are not suitable for general frying purposes, although butter is good for omelettes and cooking vegetables (see pages 27 and 50.) Pure lard is a good frying fat and some cooking fats are suitable for deep-fat frying, others can only be used for shallow frying.

How to Render Fats

Rendering means melting to extract the fat from surrounding tissues. This is what you do to extract the fat from cooked or raw pieces cut off the joint, and from bits of fat bacon or from suet.

METHOD 1. Cut the fat in small pieces and place in a pan in a slow oven until the fat has melted, and there are only crisp brown pieces of tissue left. Strain into a clean basin.

METHOD 2. Cut the pieces of fat as before, place in a pan without a lid and with a very little water. Boil until the water has been driven off and then heat very gently until the fat has melted and left only crisp brown pieces of tissue. Strain as before.

Note. — In both cases take care not to have the heat too fierce or the fat will burn and be spoilt.

How to Clarify Fat

Clarifying means cleaning. You need to clarify when you have a collection of used dripping which is mixed with gravy or specks of food and you want it clean for frying or making pastry. Frying fat must be kept clean as particles of food lower the smoking temperature (see page 59).

1. Put the fat in a saucepan without the lid and cover with water.
2. Bring to the boil and pour it into a clean basin. If a very large quantity of fat is being clarified strain the fat through fine muslin.

3. Leave until cold, when the fat will form a hard lid on top of the water and any impurities will be in the water or on the bottom of the fat.
4. Lift off the cake of fat, turn it upside down and scrape the bottom clean.
5. If the fat is to be used for cakes, pastry, puddings or spreads it may be used at this stage, but if it is wanted for frying or to be kept for some time, the water left in the fat must be removed.
6. Melt the fat in a saucepan and heat until it stops bubbling. This means that all the water has been driven off.

If the fat has a strong flavour, cook a raw sliced potato in it at this stage (6). When the potato is brown, and the fat has stopped bubbling, strain into a clean dry basin. The potato absorbs flavours.

How to Prepare Suet for Pastry

Remove any membranes and grate or chop the suet, using the coarse or medium grater (see page 13). Dredge with flour to prevent the flakes from sticking together. Packet suets are already prepared for cooking.

How to Prepare Food for Frying

Many foods need a coating either of batter, egg and breadcrumbs or of flour and milk. This coating sets when the food goes into hot fat and protects the food inside from becoming greasy. Some foods form their own coating, but may have batter or egg and breadcrumbs added for variety in flavour and appearance. Foods for which a coating is not essential are meat, raw potatoes, bacon, sausages and doughnuts.

Foods which must be coated are all mixtures using cooked potatoes, for example, rissoles, fish cakes, etc., croquettes or other mixtures of cooked food combined with a thick sauce; also fruit and cooked vegetables which are generally coated in an egg and flour batter and called "fritters". Fish is sometimes cooked without coating but it is better to dust with seasoned flour first or use one of the coatings given below.

Coating Food for Frying

Be sure the food is quite dry or the coating will not stick. It is often a help to dip the food in flour before putting it in the coating mixture.

1. **EGG AND BREADCRUMBS**. Dip the prepared food in beaten egg and make sure the whole surface is covered. A pastry brush may be used for coating. Then dip in fine breadcrumbs (see page 87) and pat well to make the crumbs stick. Use fine crumbs as coarse crumbs fall off during frying and make the fat dirty. White crumbs give a better appearance than brown crumbs.

2. **SEASONED FLOUR AND MILK**. Dip the prepared food in seasoned flour, then in milk and then in flour again. This coating is suitable for food which is to be fried in shallow fat.

3. **COATING BATTER**. Use a fairly thick batter of eggs, flour and milk or of flour and milk only. A pancake or fritter recipe is suitable. The batter must be thick enough to coat the food evenly.

Shallow or Dry Frying

This is cooking food in a frying-pan with very little fat. It is not as satisfactory as deep-fat frying, which is no more difficult to do.

1. A heavy frying-pan gives the best results.
2. Use clean fat, free from moisture as water in the fat makes it splutter when heated. (For preparing and clarifying fat, see page 60.)
3. Use enough fat to cover the bottom of the pan or come halfway up the food.
4. Have the fat very hot before adding the food. It should be heated until a very faint blue smoke rises from the surface.

5. Bacon and oily fish such as herrings or sprats may be fried without any additional fat. Heat the pan before adding the food. With bacon let the rashers overlap so that only the fat parts touch the pan.

Times required for shallow frying are the same as grilling (see page 14).

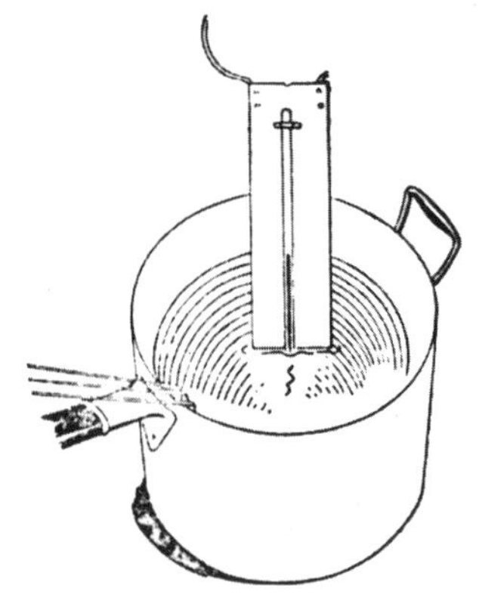

PAN, FRYING BASKET AND THERMOMETER

Deep-Fat Frying

1. Use a deep, heavy pan, for the fat must cover the food, while at the same time the pan should be only half full of fat. This is because when food is added to hot fat it bubbles violently and may boil over if the pan is too shallow. A deep pan gives better results than a wide one. Many pans sold for deep-fat frying are much too wide and shallow to be satisfactory. An ordinary saucepan is quite good provided it is of thick metal.
2. A frying basket is a help in lowering food gently into hot fat and in lifting it all out together, but it is not essential. A perforated spoon or ladle is suitable. When used for food coated in batter, it must be placed in the fat before the food is put in it.
3. For suitable fats for deep-fat frying, see page 59.
4. Heat the fat gently. When it stops bubbling and a very faint blue haze rises it is hot enough to use.

The following is a useful test: cut a 1-in. cube of stale bread and drop into the fat. If it browns in one minute the fat is hot enough for frying. If the fat smokes it is burning and will be spoilt.

If a thermometer is available the following are the correct fat temperatures for frying:

Food	*Temperature*	*Time required for cooking*
Croquettes and fish cakes	390° F.	1 minute
Chops, coated with egg and crumbs	360–400° F.	5–8 minutes
Doughnuts	360° F.	5–8 minutes
Fritters	370° F.	3–5 minutes
Fish fillets	370° F.	4–6 minutes
Fish, small whole	370° F.	3–5 minutes
Potato chips	370–390° F.	4–8 minutes

5. Do not try to fry too much food at once as this reduces the temperature of the fat and the food will not cook properly. This is why it is important to have plenty of fat in the pan.
6. Fried food should be drained on absorbent paper before serving.
7. When frying is finished strain the fat and keep for further use. If more fat is needed next time fresh fat may be added to the previous lot.

13 *Stocks, Soups and Sauces*

Stocks and Soups

Although stock is of little value as a food it is very important as an aid to well-flavoured sauces, soups, stews and other savoury dishes.

Many recipes specify "stock or water" for the liquid used in them, but it is always well worth while taking the trouble to use stock because of the extra flavour given to the dish. The best stocks are made from meat, but this is an extravagant method for small households where economy has to be considered. The following four stocks are adequate and economical. The water in which meat, poultry, fish, vegetables, rice, macaroni, etc., has been boiled should always be saved for stock.

BONE STOCK

1. Use any kind of bones, cooked or uncooked.
2. Place in a pan with cold water to cover and bring to the boil.
3. Skim and for each pint of water add 1 onion and 1 carrot. Add a bouquet garni.
4. Put the lid on and simmer very slowly for 2–3 hours or longer.
5. Strain. To remove fat, skim or leave to set and then remove.

VEGETABLE STOCK

1. Use any mixture of vegetables, outside leaves of cabbage, cauliflower stalks, outside celery stalks and leaves, green tops of leeks, watercress stalks, as well as the more usual vegetables.
2. Boil enough water to cover, chop or shred the vegetables, add to the water, cover and boil 20–30 minutes.
3. Strain and use.

EMERGENCY STOCK

Dissolve meat or yeast extract in boiling water or vegetable water.

FISH STOCK

1. Cover the fish bones, skin, head and other trimmings, with cold water. To ½ lb. of trimmings add 1 small onion, 2 cloves, ¼ bay leaf, and a small sprig of parsley.
2. Bring to the boil, cover and boil for 20 minutes.
3. Strain and use.

KEEPING STOCK

No stock will keep very long and in hot weather it should be boiled up every day to prevent it from souring. Empty it into a clean bowl or jug and do not leave it standing in the saucepan or stockpot. Stock which contains starchy foods such as flour or potatoes sours very readily.

Soups

The food value of soups depends on the ingredients used. Clear soups are of little value except to stimulate the appetite at the beginning of a meal, but the thick vegetable soups, Scotch broths, American chowders and cream soups are nourishing as well as appetising. Recipes for these are to be found in most cookery books.

Two basic methods are given below. Allow ½ pint of soup per person.

How to Make a Mixed Vegetable Soup

1. A selection of any vegetables in season should be used, allowing: ¾ lb. of vegetables to 1½ pints of stock. This will make soup for four people. Amongst the vegetables try to include onions, leeks or garlic for flavouring and at least one green leafy vegetable for Vitamin C.
2. Prepare and shred or slice the vegetables.
3. Melt enough fat to cover the bottom of the saucepan and add the vegetables.
4. Cover with a fitting lid and cook at a gentle heat for 15–20 minutes, shaking the pan occasionally to prevent sticking.
5. Add hot stock to cover and boil until the vegetables are tender. Barley, macaroni, spaghetti and noodles may be added at this stage (not more than 1 oz.).
6. Season well and serve sprinkled with grated cheese.

N.B. — If a smooth soup is required it may be rubbed through a sieve and then reheated.

How to Make a Cream Soup

Cream soups consist of a vegetable purée or pulp and a thin white sauce. They make very good supper dishes for children. Allow ½ pint of vegetable purée to 1 pint of white sauce.

1. Make the purée by cooking the vegetables in a very little water until tender.
2. Rub through a sieve and keep hot. If no sieve is available certain vegetables such as potatoes, lentils, turnips and swedes may be mashed, but the soup will not be entirely free from lumps.
3. Make a thin milk sauce (see below).
4. Add the purée to the sauce and mix well. Season and serve at once. Do not let a cream soup stand after mixing or it may curdle. If the purée was very thick the soup may need thinning with milk stock before serving.

The best vegetables to use are: peas, tomatoes, potato and leek or onion, potato and turnip, potato and watercress, swede, turnip, carrot, beans, lentils, cauliflower, celery, cucumber and pumpkin.

Sauces

Sauces may be used to add food value to a dish, for example, egg and milk sauces; but their main value is in improving the flavour, appearance and texture of other dishes.

Thickenings Used for Sauces

Flour is the best to use for all savoury sauces; cornflour, custard powder and arrowroot may be used for sweet sauces. Eggs are also used for thickening but generally combined with one of the thickening agents already mentioned.

One of the most important points to watch in sauce making is the cooking of the thickening. If the sauce is not thoroughly cooked a raw taste remains from the uncooked starch grains. Flour needs at least 5 minutes' boiling to remove the taste of raw starch; cornflour needs 10 minutes; arrowroot merely needs to be brought to the boil; and custard powder should be cooked according to the directions on the packet.

Sauces may be classified according to their thickness. ⅛ to ¼ pint of sauce should be allowed per person.

1. **A thin sauce**. Very slightly thickened, used in cream soups and sauces which are to be served cold.
2. **A pouring sauce**. Thick but will still pour very readily, used for general purposes.
3. **A thick or coating sauce**. Thicker than (1) and (2) and when poured over food it does not run off easily but coats the food thickly. Use for decoration, and for croquettes and similar mixtures.

Proportions for Thickening

(The following quantities are for 1 pint of liquid.)

Thickening Agent	*Thin Sauce*	*Pouring Sauce*	*Coating Sauce*
National Flour	½ oz.	1–1½ oz.	2 oz.
Cornflour or Arrowroot	¼ oz.	¾ oz.	1 oz.
Custard Powder	The same as cornflour or according to the directions on the packet.		

How to Make a Sauce

METHOD A (when fat is used).

1. Melt the fat (for the above quantities use 1–2 oz. fat or equal weights of fat and flour.)
2. Add the flour. (Flour is the best thickening for this method.)
3. Mix well. Cook very gently for 1–2 minutes. This mixture of fat and flour is called a roux. If brown sauce is required cook until brown.

4. Remove from the heat and add the liquid gradually. It is better for the saucepan if cold liquid is not poured into a hot pan. Either cool the pan, or heat the liquid.

Stir until smooth and boil the required time. (See page 65.) Add seasoning.

METHOD B (with or without fat.) This is the better method to use when making large quantities of sauce.
1. Mix the dry ingredients to a smooth paste with a little of the cold liquid (often called "blending", see page 10).
2. Boil the remaining liquid.
3. Pour into the blended dry ingredients, mix well and return to the pan.
4. Stir until the mixture boils. Cook for the required time. (See page 65.) Add seasoning.
5. If fat is included in the recipe add it now, but first remove the sauce from the heat. Stir until the fat melts.

How to Make Thick Gravy

1. Lift the meat from the roasting pan and keep it hot.
2. Pour off fat carefully but leave 1 tablespoon for every ½ pint of gravy required.
3. Heat the pan and when the fat is hot add 2 level tablespoons of flour for each ½ pint of gravy.
4. Mix well and cook 2 or 3 minutes.
5. Add hot stock or vegetable water. Stir until it boils. Boil 2 or 3 minutes. Season well. If necessary add a little gravy browning.

Note.—For thin gravy proceed as above but omit the flour, merely adding stock or vegetable water and seasoning to the fat in the pan.

14 *Beverages*

How to Make Tea

1. Always use water freshly drawn from the cold tap and make the tea as soon as it boils.
2. Heat the teapot thoroughly with some of the water from the kettle just before it boils. Throw this away.
3. Put in the tea, allowing 2 or more level teaspoons for each ½ pint cup of water. It is more economical to use a good brand of tea.
4. As soon as the water boils, *take the teapot to the kettle* and pour on the boiling water.

5. Allow the tea to stand for 3–5 minutes before serving. Stir well before pouring.
6. If a second cup per person is needed pour fresh boiling water on the tea leaves and infuse again. The second cup will be weaker and inferior in flavour.

How to Make Coffee

For each person allow 2 level tablespoons coffee, ½ pint freshly boiled water, pinch of salt. The method of making coffee depends on the equipment available. The best coffee is made from freshly roasted and freshly ground beans. If it is some time since the coffee was ground, heat it gently for a few minutes in a dry pan on top of the stove or in the oven before adding the water.

DRIP METHOD

METHOD 1 — using a jug. A coarse, ground coffee is the best to use for this method. Warm the jug. Add coffee and salt. Pour in boiling water and stand in a warm place for about 15 minutes. It is a good plan to stand the jug in a saucepan of boiling water. Stir the coffee and let it settle again. Strain and reheat if necessary, but do not boil. For straining use a very fine wire coffee strainer or a piece of fine muslin.

METHOD 2 — using a saucepan. A coarsely ground coffee is the best to use for this method.

Put the water, coffee and salt in the pan and just bring to the boil. Stand in a warm place for about 15 minutes. Stir and let it settle again. Strain and reheat as above.

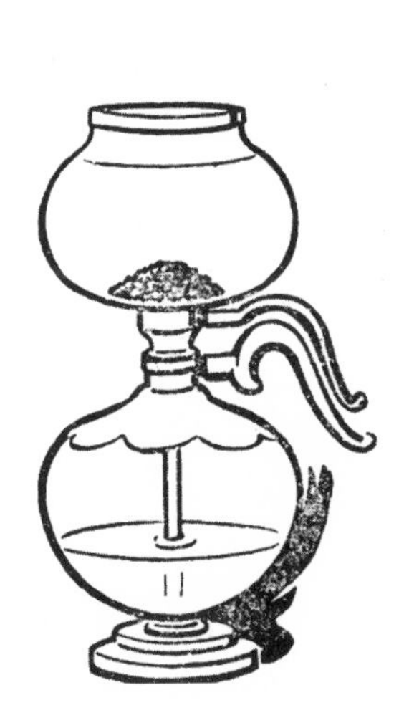

VACUUM TYPE

METHOD 3 — drip method. A fine or medium ground coffee is the best.

Special types of coffee pots are sold for this method. The ground coffee is placed in the top compartment in the strainer provided and boiling water is poured on a little at a time. The coffee drips through into the jug below. Stand the coffee pot in a pan of boiling water to keep the coffee hot. The whole process takes about 20 minutes.

The same method may be used with a piece of muslin in a strainer over the top of a saucepan. Place the coffee in the muslin and pour on boiling water, a little at a time.

The drip method is also used in the vacuum type of coffee pot. The ground coffee is placed on the filter in the top compartment, the water is placed in the lower compartment and heated until it bubbles up the tube into the top. Remove from the heat, stir well, and leave until the coffee has filtered down below. Remove the top and serve.

PERCOLATOR

METHOD 4 — using a percolator. A fine or medium ground coffee is best.

1. Place the coffee in the proper compartment.
2. Put the correct quantity of hot or cold water in the bottom of the percolator and bring to the boil.
3. Keep boiling sufficiently rapidly for the liquid to syphon up and over the ground coffee.
4. The time to allow depends on the amount of coffee being made. Ten minutes should be sufficient for coffee for four people. Count the time from the moment the water begins to syphon over the coffee.

N.B. — It is most important to keep all equipment used in coffee making perfectly clean. Wash well immediately after use, dry and leave to air.

How to Make Cocoa

METHOD 1 — using fresh milk.
For each cup allow: 2 level teaspoons cocoa.
1 level teaspoon sugar or to taste.
Pinch of salt.
½ pint milk or milk and water.

1. Mix cocoa, sugar, and salt to a smooth paste with some of the cold liquid.
2. Boil the remaining liquid and pour it into the cocoa and sugar.
3. Return this mixture to the pan and allow to boil for 1–2 minutes before serving. This boiling is important for it cooks the starch present in cocoa and gives it a much better flavour.

METHOD 2 — using household milk or other dried milk.
For each ½ pint cup allow: 2 ½ level tablespoons household milk.
1 level teaspoon sugar.
2 level teaspoons cocoa.
½ pint water.

1. Mix milk, sugar and cocoa to a smooth paste with a little cold water.
2. Add remaining water, boiling, and stir well.
3. It is an improvement to boil this 1–2 minutes as with Method 1.

Storing Coffee, Tea and Cocoa

These should be kept in airtight containers. It is better to buy small quantities to avoid loss of flavour.

15 *Cereals, Cereal Products and Starch*

Cereals are the seeds of grasses. Those most commonly used for food are wheat, barley, rice, oats, rye and corn.

Cereal products are the foods made from cereals, for example, flour, semolina (from wheat), oatmeal (from oats), cornflour (from maize), macaroni, spaghetti, vermicelli and noodles. These last four are made from wheat and are often called pastas.

Starch foods are made from the starchy roots or stems of certain plants, for example, sago, tapioca and arrowroot.

STORING CEREALS. Keep them in covered jars and inspect them every two or three weeks to make sure they are in good condition.

Cooking Cereals and Starches

When these are mixed with water or other liquid and heated the starch grains of which they are made soften and swell. This makes the grains more digestible and improves the flavour. As the grain swells it absorbs water and this accounts for its thickening powers. Cereals are used for the following purposes:

1. Thickening sauces (see page 65).
2. Making moulds, rice, oatmeal, semolina, sago (see page 70).
3. Making baked milk puddings such as rice pudding, tapioca, sago (see page 70).
4. As an accompaniment to meat and savoury dishes, rice, macaroni, etc.
5. For porridge — oatmeal and rolled oats.
6. For bread, pastry, cakes and puddings. Wheat flour is most generally used, but oatmeal, cornflour, arrowroot and semolina are also used for special dishes.

How to Make a Mould with Rice, Oatmeal, Semolina or Sago

The following are the proportions for 1 pint of liquid, sufficient for four portions:

Food	*Amount*	*Boiling Time*
Rice	2 oz.	15–20 minutes
Oatmeal	3 oz.	15–20 minutes
Semolina	3 oz.	5 minutes
Sago	2 oz.	15–20 minutes.

1. Boil the milk or other liquid and when boiling sprinkle in the cereal.
2. Stir well and boil gently for the required time. If milk is used and there is danger of it catching, cook the cereal over boiling water (i.e., in a double sauce-pan or in a basin in a saucepan) after it has begun to thicken. In that case the cooking time will be about half as long again.
3. Add the flavouring and sweetening and pour into the mould which has been rinsed with cold water and not dried.
4. Leave to set and turn out. The mould may easily be loosened from the edges by pulling away with the fingers.

How to Make a Mould with Cornflour or Arrowroot

Allow 1–1½ oz. per pint of liquid, enough for four portions.
1. Mix the cornflour or arrowroot to a smooth paste with a little of the cold liquid.
2. Boil the remaining liquid and pour it into the blended mixture. Stir well.
3. Return to the pan and stir until it boils. Boil 10 minutes for cornflour. If milk is used see paragraph 2 under "How to Make a Mould with Rice".
4. Add flavouring and sugar and pour into a mould, as with rice.

How to Make Baked Milk Puddings Using Rice, Tapioca, Sago and Barley

The following are the proportions to use for 1 pint of milk — enough for three to four portions:

Food	*Amount*	*Baking Time*
Rice	1 ½ oz.	2 hours
Tapioca	1 ½ oz.	1 hour
Sago	1 ½ oz.	1 hour
Pearl Barley	1 ½ oz.	2 hours

1. Place the cereal in a pie dish with 1 oz. of sugar and flavouring.
2. Add the milk and, if liked, a grating of nutmeg on top.
3. Bake in a slow oven, 250° F. to 350° F. It is the long slow baking which makes a milk pudding creamy and rich.

How to Boil Rice

There are many different ways recommended for boiling rice, but the following simple method gives excellent results:

1. Use plenty of water and if the rice is required for savoury dishes add salt to the water. (Use 1½–2 pints of water, and 1 level tablespoon of salt to each 2 oz. of rice.)
2. Boil the water and add the rice gradually so that the water does not go off the boil.
3. Do not cover with the lid. Keep boiling rapidly. This keeps the grains of rice constantly moving so that they have no chance to stick to the bottom of the pan, or to each other. (See diagram opposite.)

4. Boil until the rice is just tender. The time varies from 5–15 minutes according to the kind of rice, but it is most important not to overcook. Properly cooked rice should have each grain separate. To test if the rice is cooked, squeeze a grain between the thumb and first finger. If it is cooked it will be soft; if uncooked, there will be a hard particle of starch in the centre of the grain.

5. Strain the rice, if possible, on a wide shallow cook's sieve, return to the pan and stand on a warm place to dry out, or spread on a wire tray in a cool oven.

How to Boil Macaroni, Spaghetti, etc.

These foods, which are known generally as "pastas", are cooked in the following manner:

1. Allow plenty of water (1 quart of water to 4 oz. macaroni). Add one level tablespoon of salt to each quart of water and bring to the boil.
2. Macaroni and spaghetti may be cooked whole or broken into short lengths. Add to the boiling salted water. Do not cover the pan.
3. Boil until tender. The time varies depending on the type of pasta being used but it is important to boil until just tender and to avoid over-cooking. If over-cooked the pasta clings together in a sticky mess.
4. Drain and rinse with cold water.
5. Reheat in the sauce or liquid with which it is to be served or use in made-up dishes.

How to Make Oatmeal Porridge

There are several methods of making porridge according to the equipment available and to personal tastes. The following are three of the methods:
4 oz. medium oatmeal, 2 pints water, a pinch of salt; for four people.

METHOD 1
Soak the oatmeal in the water overnight. Next morning add salt, bring to the boil and cook for 15–20 minutes, stirring occasionally to prevent sticking.

METHOD 2
A hay box may be used for cooking porridge. If this method is used, boil the water and salt, sprinkle in the oatmeal, stirring well. Cook for 5 minutes, then transfer to a hay box and leave for at least 1½ hours or overnight if preferred. Reheat before serving.

METHOD 3
Boil the water and salt. Sprinkle in the oatmeal, stirring quickly all the time. Boil for 5 minutes and serve.

16 *Sugar*

The following sugars are used in cooking:

Castor, granulated, loaf, pieces, Demerara, Barbados and icing sugar, treacle, golden syrup, honey, maple syrup and glucose. Jam has a high percentage of sugar and is used in cooking in place of sugar.

Storing Sugar

Keep it in covered jars. Jam should be kept in a cool, dry, airy cupboard to avoid mould.

The Effect of Heat on Sugar

When granulated, loaf or castor sugar is heated it first of all melts and then changes in colour from white to pale brown and then to dark brown, which is called "caramel". It then has a characteristic toffee flavour and is used in certain sweets and puddings, for example, Crême Caramel and Caramel Rice.

Temperatures Used in Sweet Making

The following terms are referred to in recipes for sweets, candies and boiled icings. Different kinds of sweets are obtained by boiling the sugar and liquid to different stages and it is important to follow the instructions in the recipe exactly.

A sugar thermometer is a great help and the same thermometer may be used in deep-fat frying (see page 62).

When sugar and water are heated together they first of all form a syrup and then, if boiling is continued, the following stages are reached:

1. **THREAD STAGE**. 230° F. When a little syrup is dropped from a spoon a very fine thread is seen.

2. **SOFT BALL STAGE**. 236° F. When a little syrup is dropped into cold water it can be formed into a soft ball with the fingers.

3. **HARD BALL STAGE**. 254° F. As in (2) but a hard ball is formed.

4. **THE CRACK OR BRITTLE STAGE**. 290° F. The syrup immediately hardens and crackles when dropped into cold water.

5. **CARAMEL STAGE**. 350° F. When the syrup turns brown.

17 *Batters, Cakes and Pastry*

These are mixtures of flour, sugar, eggs, fat, liquid and flavourings in varying proportions. They are often classified according to the consistency of the mixture and in the following recipes it is essential to understand what is meant by the different terms.

SOFT DOUGH STIFF DOUGH

STIFF MIXTURE

Doughs

1. "Mix to a stiff dough" means add just enough liquid to bind the ingredients together, for example, pastry and most biscuits.
2. "Mix to a soft dough" means add liquid to make a mixture which is as soft as possible without being too soft to handle easily and knead or roll out, for example, scones and yeast dough. Yeast doughs are sometimes called "elastic" after kneading, that is, if pressed with the finger the dent quickly disappears. Doughs other than yeast should not be mixed or kneaded to this stage or they will be tough when baked.

Cake and Pudding Mixtures

3. "A stiff mixture" or consistency means a

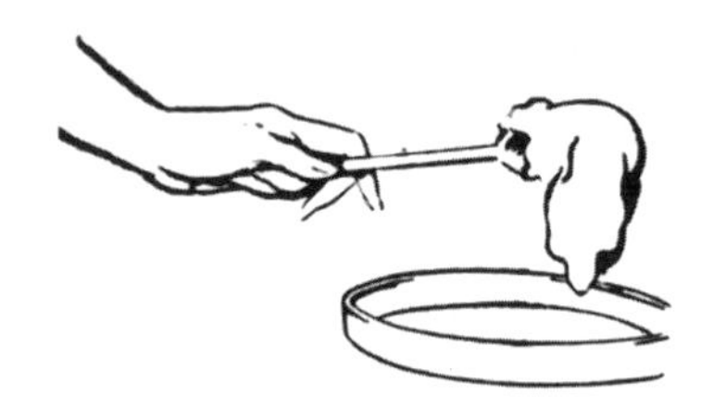

SOFT MIXTURE

little more liquid than the soft dough. Too sticky to handle, but stiff enough to keep its shape when dropped from a spoon, for example, rock cakes.

4. "A soft mixture" or consistency means a mixture which drops from the spoon in lumps but is too thick to pour, for example, most cake mixtures.

Batters

THICK BATTER

5. "A thick batter" means a pouring mixture the consistency of very thick cream, for example, drop scones or Scotch pancakes. The batter spreads slowly when dropped from a spoon.

6. "A thin batter" means a pouring mixture the consistency of thin cream, for example, Yorkshire pudding or pancakes. The batter spreads quickly in a thin layer when dropped from a spoon or poured from a jug.

THIN BATTER

What Makes Batters, Cakes and Doughs Light?

1. Cold air beaten or folded in during mixing. The air expands when the mixture is heated and lightens the dough or batter. The following mixtures depend entirely on air for making them light: pastry of all kinds (unless self-raising flour is used); true sponges made with fresh eggs; cream puffs and éclairs; Yorkshire pudding and pancakes; meringues.

2. Carbon dioxide, a gas which expands on heating in the same way as air. Carbon dioxide is produced in the following ways:

(a) By using bicarbonate of soda with something containing acid such as sour milk, golden syrup, treacle, or cream of tartar. This is not a very accurate method as the amount of acid present in milk or syrup is very variable.

(b) By adding baking powder or golden raising powder. These consist of an alkali and an acid. The quality is controlled by law so that the baking powder and golden raising powder must be capable of producing a certain amount of carbon dioxide. This is the most accurate method of raising mixtures. All powders should be kept dry in airtight jars or tins as they quicky deteriorate if allowed to become damp.

(c) By using yeast which feeds on the sugar in mixtures and produces carbon dioxide.

Proportions of Raising Agent to Use with National Flour

1. BAKING POWDER

A good standard to take is 4 level teaspoons baking powder to ½ lb. of flour. (For level measures see page 18.) The amount can be reduced if eggs are beaten into the mixture, but more baking powder is needed when using dried eggs than fresh; a recipe where the fat is rubbed in needs more baking powder than one which is creamed; and cakes with very little fat and sugar need more than richer cakes.

2. BICARBONATE OF SODA AND AN ACID SUBSTANCE

1 level teaspoon of soda with ½ pint of sour milk = 4 level teaspoons of baking powder.
1 level teaspoon of soda with ¾ lb. golden syrup = 4 level teaspoons of baking powder.
1 level teaspoon of soda with 2½ level teaspoons of cream of tartar = 4 level teaspoons of baking powder.

If an excess of soda is used the finished product will have a bitter taste and may have yellow or green spots throughout.

N.B.—All raising agents should be very carefully mixed with the flour. It is better to sift them all together. Soda may be dissolved in the liquid.

The Kinds of Flour Used in Baking

Wheat flour is the one most commonly used. Flour contains a protein substance called "gluten". When moistened and beaten gluten becomes elastic and this helps to hold the air or carbon dioxide in the mixture and make it light. Different kinds of wheat have different amounts and kinds of gluten. It is important to buy a good quality flour, and for cakes and pastry one which has been specially prepared from the right kinds of wheat. A flour which is good for bread-making is not generally satisfactory for cakes. If a bread flour only is available it is a help when making cakes to mix some cornflour, arrowroot, or soya flour with it in the proportion of a ¼ lb. to ¾ lb. of the flour.

Cakes made entirely from cornflour, arrowroot, rice flour, potato flour or soya flour are not satisfactory. Barley, rye and oatmeal also give better results if used with wheat flour. Wholemeal flour can be used for making cakes and pastry but the results are coarse in texture.

Self-raising flour has the raising agent already added. It is suitable for plain cakes and scones or any recipe in which a fairly large amount of raising agent is needed. It is not suitable for rich fruit cakes.

Tips on Mixing Batters

1. Mix the dry ingredients with just enough liquid to make a thick smooth batter. Then beat very thoroughly.
2. Add remaining liquid and beat again.
3. It is not necessary to leave a batter to stand before baking.
4. When using dried eggs add them dry to the flour.
5. When using dried milk add it dry to the flour and mix the batter with water.

Cake and Pudding Mixtures

These may be divided into three groups depending on the method of mixing.

1. SPONGES.

A true sponge consists of eggs, sugar, flour and flavouring. It depends for its lightness on the air which is beaten into the eggs. Sometimes a little melted fat is added after the flour has been mixed in.

IMPORTANT POINTS IN MIXING SPONGES.

(a) See that the eggs and sugar are very thoroughly beaten. They should be so thick and light that when the beater is withdrawn the mixture takes some time to level out again (see page 26).

(b) The flour should be well sifted and folded in very lightly (see page 12, "Cut and Fold").

(c) Any liquid or melted fat should be added last and folded in very gently.

(d) Sponge tins should be greased well and dusted with flour.

(e) A sponge is cooked if, when pressed lightly with the finger, the impression springs back immediately. (For temperatures see page 86.)

(f) Handle the sponge very carefully and do not tap or bang the tin. Run a knife round the edge to loosen the cake, invert the tin and let the sponge fall out with its own weight. Sponge rolls should be turned out on to a cloth or greaseproof paper sprinkled with sugar. Spread on the filling and roll up at once.

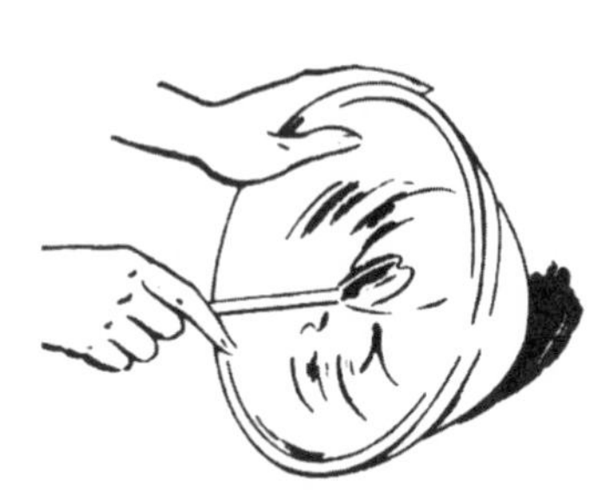

2. CREAMED MIXTURES.

The fat and sugar are beaten together with the eggs and when the mixture is light the flour and liquid are added.

IMPORTANT POINTS TO WATCH:

(a) Cream the fat and sugar very thoroughly. Soften the fat slightly first and then beat in the sugar. The mixture should be smooth, light and fluffy and look like whipped cream. If shell eggs are used beat them separately until they are very thick and light. Stir them into the creamed mixture either just before the flour or alternately with it. Dried eggs may be added dry and the water needed for reconstituting them beaten in gradually. To prevent curdling the creamed mixture it is a good plan to add only half the water at this stage and mix in the rest with the flour.

(b) Any flavouring essences should be added after creaming.

(c) Add the flour, baking powder, spices, salt, etc., sifted together. Stir them in with a circular motion and do not beat. Mix until the ingredients are smoothly blended. Add any liquid with the flour.

(d) Fruit is added last and stirred in gently.

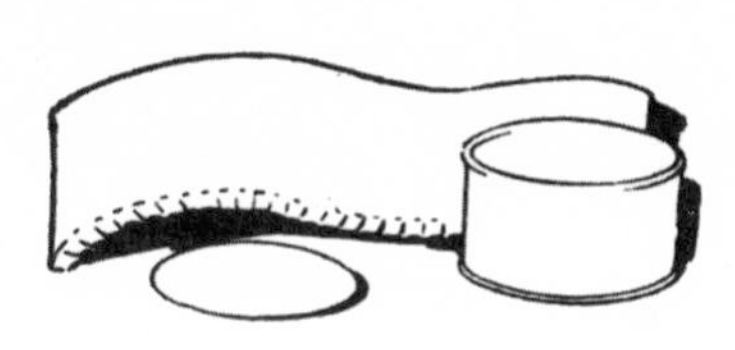

PAPER LINING FOR CAKE TIN

(e) Grease the cake tins and dust with a little flour or line them with greaseproof paper. To do this cut a piece of paper the size of the bottom of the tin. Then cut a strip to go round the sides of the tin and a little deeper than its height. Bend up ½ in. along the bottom edge and snip closely with scissors. This will make the paper lie flat in the bottom of the tin. Put this piece in first and then the bottom piece of paper lies over the nicked edge and makes a perfectly flat lining.

(f) Fill tins only two-thirds full to allow for rising and make a slight depression in the middle so that it will rise flat.

(g) To test whether a cake is cooked insert a fine skewer or a steel knitting needle. If the skewer comes out clean, that is, with no uncooked cake clinging to it, the cake is done. If the cake shrinks from the sides of the tin this also shows it is cooked.

(h) Leave the cake to cool a minute or two before turning it out and it will then come out more easily. Handle carefully.

3. RUBBED IN MIXTURES.

In this method the fat is rubbed into the flour, salt and baking powder, and then the other dry ingredients added and the whole mixed to the correct consistency with milk or other liquid. The eggs may be beaten and added with the liquid, or if dried eggs are used they may be added dry with the other dry ingredients and the water needed for reconstitution added with the mixing liquid.

The important part of mixing these cakes is to rub the fat in very thoroughly (see "Short Pastry", page 80).

For the preparation of tins and baking see above, "Creamed Mixtures".

What Should a Good Cake Look Like?

1. It should have a smooth top and be baked an even brown, top, bottom and sides.

2. It should rise well with the top slightly rounded towards the centre. It should not be peaked or cracked. Many cooks think a cake should crack on top, but if this happens the cake is never as soft, light and moist as when it is made with a level or slightly rounded top.

3. It should have a fine even texture with no large holes or tunnels and no lumps of unmixed flour.

Common Faults in Cake Making and Their Causes

UNEVEN RISING may be due to:
1. Baking too quickly.
2. The cake being placed to one side of the oven.
3. Too much flour being used.
4. Too much baking powder or other raising agent being used.

A COARSE, OPEN TEXTURE may be due to:
1. Insufficient creaming of the fat, sugar and eggs.
2. Careless mixing after the flour has been added.
3. Too slow an oven.
4. Too much baking powder or other raising agent used.

A CAKE SINKING IN THE MIDDLE during or after cooking may be due to:
1. Too slow an oven.
2. Insufficient flour.
3. Moving the cake while it was still rising and before it had set.
4. The wrong proportions of fat and sugar.
5. Too much baking powder or other raising agent.
6. Not cooking long enough.

A DRY CAKE may be due to:
1. Too low a temperature.
2. Cooking the cake too long.
3. Making the mixture too stiff.

A HEAVY CAKE may be due to:
1. Too much fat.
2. Too much flour.
3. Over-mixing the cake after the flour was added.
4. Too much liquid.
5. Not cooking long enough or cooking too slowly.

TUNNELS IN A CAKE may be due to:
1. Too hot an oven.
2. Too much flour.
3. Too much baking soda in mixtures using soda and cream of tartar or golden syrup or sour milk.
4. Over-mixing of the cake after the flour was added.

A SUGARY CRUST may be due to:
1. Too slow an oven.
2. Too much sugar.

FRUIT SINKING may be due to:
1. Too much raising agent.
2. Not enough flour used.
3. Damp fruit.

N.B.—All the above possibilities show how important it is to follow good recipes very carefully and weigh and measure all ingredients exactly.

Steamed Puddings

Most modern steamed puddings are made by one or other of the cake-mixing methods already described and the same rules apply.

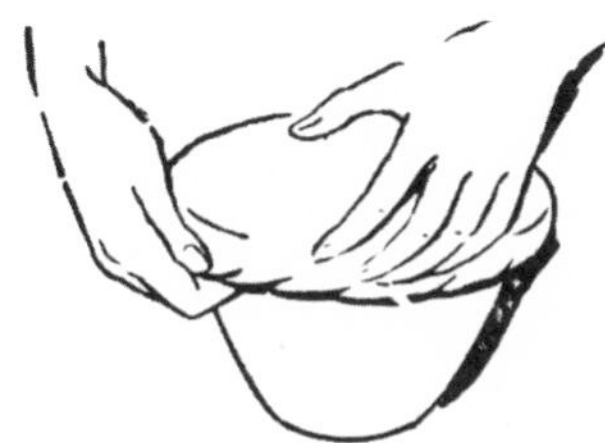

How to Steam a Pudding

METHOD A. Where the pudding is cooked in a steamer over boiling water.

1. Place the pudding mixture in a greased basin, filling it about two-thirds full, thus leaving room for the pudding to rise.
2. Cover the top with greased paper.
3. Have plenty of water in the lower half of the steamer and keep it boiling rapidly to provide plenty of steam.
4. Place the pudding in the steamer, place the lid on the steamer and steam for the required length of time, as given in the recipe.
5. It may be necessary to add a little extra water from time to time. Add boiling water so as not to hinder the steaming process.

METHOD A.

METHOD B.

1. The pudding is prepared as before but instead of using a steamer the pudding basin is placed in a saucepan containing boiling water to come half-way up the sides of the basin. Put the lid on the pan.
2. Keep the water boiling gently for the required length of time as given in the recipe.

METHOD B.

Boiled Puddings

The only puddings which are boiled in present-day cooking are roly-poly suet puddings. (For suet pastry, see page 82.) Even these may be steamed if a steamer is available.

1. Place the mixture in a floured cloth. Roll up like a sausage and tie loosely at each end, leaving room for the pudding to rise. Use a thick firm cloth, such as calico.
2. Place the pudding in a saucepan with boiling water to cover. Put on the lid.
3. Keep the water boiling during the whole of the cooking time, generally 2–2½ hours.

Soft Doughs

Yeast mixtures are slower to make and require more attention than baking powder mixtures. They are seldom attempted by the beginner and will not be dealt with here. Of the soft doughs, scones are the most frequently made and the following points are important.

How to Make Scones

1. Sift the dry ingredients together. Many cooks favour the use of bicarbonate of soda and cream of tartar instead of baking powder for scones, but unless the quantities are measured very carefully the flavour may be spoiled by the bitter taste of too much soda.
2. Rub in the fat very thoroughly, using the tips of the fingers. (See "Short Pastry", below.)
3. Mix in the milk or other liquid, using a knife or palette knife and tossing the mixture lightly. Add liquid to make a soft dough (see page 73).
4. Turn on to a lightly floured board or table and pat with the hands or roll to about ½ in. thick.
5. Cut in shapes and bake in a very hot oven for 10–15 minutes. The tops may be brushed with beaten egg or milk before baking. It is better to roll the scones fairly thinly, about ½"– ¾" as if they are made thick the outside tends to become overcooked before the inside is done.

Stiff Doughs
Pastry Making: What Makes Pastry Tough and Hard?

1. Too little fat for the amount of flour.
2. Too much water, that is, too soft a dough (see page 73).
3. Too much kneading and rolling.
4. Too slow an oven for baking.

How to Make Short Pastry

Short pastry is used for pies, tarts, turnovers and pasties.

1. Weigh or measure ingredients carefully. Sift the flour and salt to remove lumps and mix in air.
2. Allow 2½–4 oz. fat to 8 oz. flour. When using less fat than half the weight of flour, that is less than 4 oz. fat to 8 oz. flour, some people find it a help to add a little baking powder (1 level teaspoon to 8 oz. flour).
3. Lard or cooking fat makes the shortest pastry, and consequently less is required for the same results. A mixture of half lard or cooking fat and half margarine is very good. Clarified dripping may be used but beef dripping makes a shorter crust than hard mutton fat.

4. Rub the fat into the flour, using the tips of the fingers, lifting the hands up out of the basin. Rub until the mixture looks like fine bread-crumbs.
5. Mix with cold water and add only enough water to bind the ingredients into a very stiff dough. Too much water and a soft mixture makes a hard, tough pastry. Do not knead the pastry as this helps to make it tough.
6. Flour the pastry board or table very lightly. If it is found necessary to keep on flouring the board and rolling pin the pastry is too wet. Roll lightly and do not handle more than is necessary.

When scraps of pastry have to be re-rolled place the pieces in layers one on top of each other and roll out. Do not knead them together or the pastry will be tough.

7. If possible leave the pastry to stand in a cool place for 15–30 minutes before baking. This should always be done with pastry which has been rolled twice. The standing helps to prevent the pastry from being tough.
8. Use a hot oven. Too low a temperature gives poor rising and a hard pastry. For temperatures see page 86.

How to Make Rough Flaky Pastry

This pastry is simpler to make than real flaky pastry and gives good results. It is suitable for meat pies, fruit pies, patties and any purpose for which flaky pastry is normally used.

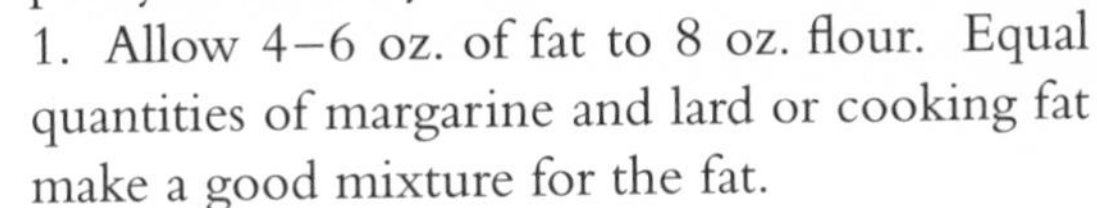

1. Allow 4–6 oz. of fat to 8 oz. flour. Equal quantities of margarine and lard or cooking fat make a good mixture for the fat.
2. Have everything as cold as possible.
3. Sift the flour and salt and cut in the fat by using two knives like scissor blades in a bowl and cutting in the fat in small flakes.
4. When the fat is in small pieces the size of a pea, mix the pastry to a stiff dough with very cold water.
5. Roll out into a rectangle about ¼ in. thick, keeping the ends square and the sides even.
6. Fold the pastry by bringing the side edges to the middle, then the top and bottom edges to the middle, fold in half, and press the edges together.

7. To roll the pastry again give it a half-turn so that the unbroken edge is on your right-hand side. Roll out and use as required. It is a great help if the pastry can be put in a very cold place to "rest" in between the first and second rollings.

How to Make Hot Water Pastry or "Raised" Pies

This pastry is mixed hot and moulded into shape with the hands. It is used for meat pies such as pork, veal and ham, and so on. It is economical of fat, using 2 to 3 oz. lard or cooking fat for ½ lb. flour. Allow ¼ pint hot water for this quantity and 1 level teaspoon of salt.

1. Warm the flour and salt in a basin.
2. Put the fat and water in a pan and bring to the boil.
3. Pour into the flour and mix well with a wooden spoon.
4. Knead with the hands until all cracks disappear and the mixture is smooth and pliable.
5. Use while still warm and mould to line a greased tin or special pie mould. A small loaf pan is a good shape for one of these pies.
6. Add the filling, generally uncooked, and cover with a lid of pastry. Make a hole in the centre and decorate.
7. Meat pies made this way are best cooked in a moderate oven for 1–2 hours. When the pie is cooked fill up with hot stock and if the pie is to be eaten cold add gelatine to the stock.

How to Make Suet Pastry

This is used for steamed and boiled puddings, such as steak and kidney pudding, apple pudding and other fruit puddings, jam roly-poly, and dumplings.

1. Beef suet is the best, but suet from lamb or mutton may be used. If no suet is available grated clarified mutton dripping may be used instead. Use 3 oz. fat to 8 oz. flour.
2. Sift together the flour, salt (1 level teaspoon to 8 oz. flour) and baking powder (2 level teaspoons).
3. The suet should be grated (see page 13), or finely chopped, and added to the dry ingredients.
4. Add enough water to make a soft dough (see page 73) but not a sticky one. When mixed the dough should leave the sides of the basin quite clean.
5. Roll and use as required. (To line a basin see page 86.)

How to Make a Flan

1. Roll the pastry to a circle ⅛ in.–¼ in. thick and 2 in. wider than the ring.
2. Place the flan ring on a baking tray and ease the pastry into the ring, taking care not to stretch it. Press to fit bottom and sides carefully so that no air bubbles form underneath the crust.
3. Roll across the top of the ring with the rolling pin to press away any overlapping pastry.
4. The edge may be left plain or pinched with the fingers to form a fluting.

5. If the flan is being baked without a filling, prick the bottom well or put in two or three crusts to prevent it from rising. Bake in a hot oven for 15–20 minutes for an empty shell, 30–40 minutes for a filled shell, depending on the filling used.
6. Lift off the baking tray and remove the ring.

Note.—If a flan ring is not available use a sandwich tin and line it in the same way.

How to Make a Double Crust Tart

Double crust tarts may be made in flan rings or sandwich tins, but are more easily handled if made in a deep plate of enamel, tin, or heat resistant glass.

1. Roll a circular piece of pastry to ⅛ in. thick and 1 in. to 2 in. wider than the plate.

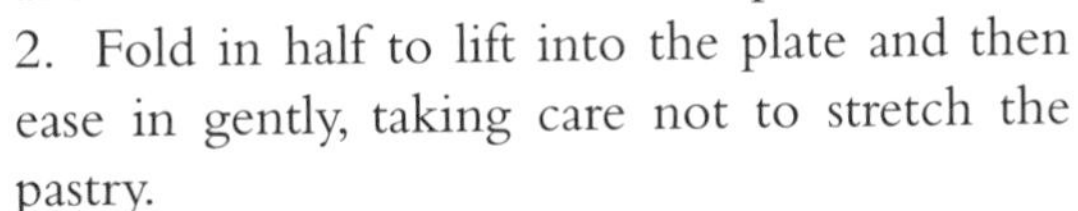

2. Fold in half to lift into the plate and then ease in gently, taking care not to stretch the pastry.
3. Trim the overhanging edges so that they are even with the rim of the plate.

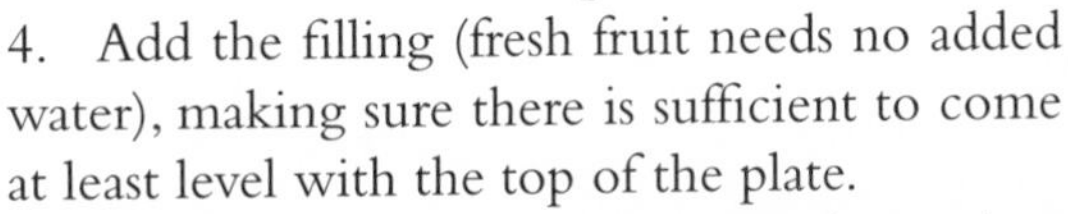

4. Add the filling (fresh fruit needs no added water), making sure there is sufficient to come at least level with the top of the plate.

5. Roll another piece of pastry 2 in. larger than the plate.
6. Moisten the edge of the pie and lift the top on. Ease it into position without stretching.
7. Fold the overhanging upper crust over the lower and flute the edges by using the first finger of one hand to dent the pastry on the

outside and pinching the dent to a sharp point with the first finger and thumb of the other hand from the inside. Cut a slit in the centre to allow the steam to escape.

8. Brush the top with milk or beaten egg or white of egg and sifted sugar and bake in a hot oven for ½–¾ of an hour, depending on the kind of filling used.

How to Make an Open Tart

These are used for the same purpose as flan cases. Many cooks find them easier to handle as the tart may be served in the deep plate in which it was cooked. Enamel, tin or heat resistant glass plates are suitable.

1. Try to keep the pastry circular and roll it about ⅛ in. thick and 3 to 4 in. wider than the plate.
2. Fold the pastry in half to lift it into the plate. Ease it in gently, taking care not to stretch it.
3. Trim the edges with a sharp knife or a pair of kitchen scissors, leaving 1½ in. hanging over.
4. Fold the overhanging pastry underneath the rest to make it level with the edge of the plate. Then bend the thickened edge upright.
5. Flute the edge as in the double crust tart.
6. If the tart is being baked without a filling prick the bottom well or put in two or three crusts to prevent it from rising. Bake in a hot oven 15–20 minutes for an empty shell, 30–40 minutes if the filling has been added.

How to Make a Lattice Top

1. Proceed as above in "How to Make an Open Tart", for stages 1, 2 and 3, but trim the pastry level with the edge of the plate. Then put the filling in the tart.
2. Cut strips of pastry ⅛ in. thick and ¼ in.–½ in. wide. Brush the edge of the tart with water and lay the strips criss-cross over the filling, pressing the ends well into the edge of the pastry. The strips may be twisted as a spiral.
3. Cut a strip about ¼ in. wide, and lay all round the edge to cover the ends of the criss-cross strips.
4. Press edges together with a fork. Bake in a hot oven for 20–30 minutes.

How to Cover a Pie

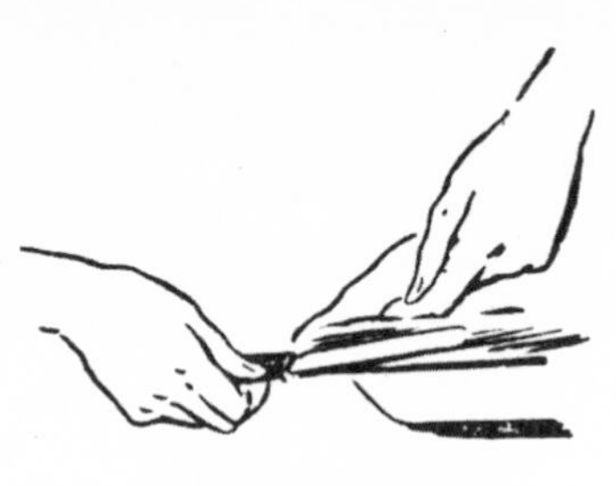

SLASHING THE EDGE.

SCALLOPING THE EDGE.

1. Fill the pie dish well, and if the contents are likely to shrink considerably during cooking, use a pie funnel or inverted egg cup to hold up the crust.
2. Roll the pastry about ¼ in. thick and about 1 in. wider than the top. Cut a strip of pastry the width and length of the edge of the pie dish. Damp the edge of the dish and lay the pastry on. Damp this pastry on top.
3. Place the large piece of pastry over the rolling pin to lift it and lay it gently on top of the pie, taking care not to stretch it. Press down at the edges.
4. Trim off the surplus. Flute the edge (see page 83) or press with a fork or flake by slashing the edge of the pastry horizontally with a knife, and then scalloping. Cut a slit in the centre of the crust to let out steam. If a pie funnel has been used the slit should come over it.
5. Brush with egg or milk or egg white and sifted sugar and bake in a hot oven ½ hour or longer according to the kind of pie (see page 86).

N.B.—For fruit pies add ¼ pint liquid to every 2 lb. fruit. For meat pies add water three-quarters of the way up the dish.

How to Line a Basin with Pastry

Suet pastry is generally used for lining a basin to make fruit pudding, steak and kidney puddings, etc., but an economical short pastry recipe may be used.

1. Keep one quarter of the pastry for the top and roll the rest into a circle ¼ in. to ½ in. thick.
2. Lift it gently into the basin, easing and not stretching. Press to fit the sides and bottom and overhang the top 1 in. all round.
3. Add the filling which should be sufficient to come to the top of the basin.
4. Roll the remaining quarter of pastry into a circle to fit the top of the basin and place it on top of the filling.
5. Moisten the edges, fold the bottom crust on top and press the edges together.
6. Cover with greased paper and steam (see page 79) for the required length of time, generally two hours or more.

Biscuits

The methods of mixing may be any of those described for cakes, but the mixture is made as stiff as pastry. It may be necessary to use the hands to work in the flour to make a smooth dough. The important points with biscuits are first of all to roll them thinly and evenly and to cut them all the same size. Otherwise they will bake unevenly. Secondly bake them slowly so that they are crisp or they will not keep well. Do not put away until they are quite cold and then store them in an airtight tin.

Baking Time-table

(For definitions of temperatures see page 16.)

Food	*Temperature*	*Time*
PASTRY		
Fruit pie	425° F.–475° F.	35–45 minutes
Meat pie–uncooked filling	375° F.–400° F.	1½–2 hours
Meat pie–cooked filling	425° F.–475° F.	30–40 minutes
Fruit tart (in deep plate)	450° F.–475° F.	35–50 minutes
Flaky pastry (patties, etc.)	475° F.–500° F.	10–20 minutes
Choux pastry (cream puffs)	450° F.–475° F.	30–40 minutes
Flan case	450° F.–500° F.	10–20 minutes
Jam tarts	450° F.–500° F.	10–15 minutes
Cornish pasties	450° F.–500° F.	30–40 minutes
CAKES AND BISCUITS		
Biscuits	350° F.–400° F.	15–30 minutes
Small cakes	400° F.–450° F.	15–20 minutes
Plain fruit cakes	350° F.–400° F.	Depends on size
Rich fruit cake	250° F.–350° F.	Depends on size
Madeira cake	350° F.–400° F.	Depends on size
Gingerbread	350° F.–400° F.	Depends on size
Sponge roll	400° F.–450° F.	8–10 minutes
Sponge sandwich (fresh eggs)	350° F.–400° F.	20–30 minutes
Sponge sandwich (dried eggs)	400° F.–450° F.	15–20 minutes
Victoria sandwich	400° F.–450° F.	15–30 minutes
Cookies and Drop cakes	400° F.–450° F.	15–30 minutes
Rock cakes	425° F.–450° F.	15–30 minutes
Scones	475° F.–500° F.	8–15 minutes
PUDDINGS		
Baked custard	350° F.–400° F.	45 minutes to 1 hour
Rice pudding	250° F.–350° F.	2 hours
Yorkshire pudding	475° F.–500° F.	35–45 minutes
Bread pudding	375° F.–425° F.	45 minutes to 1 hour
Meringues	250° F.–300° F.	1½–2 hours
Souffle	425° F.–475° F.	12–20 minutes
Meringues on pudding or tart	400° F.–425° F.	12–18 minutes

18 *Bread and Sandwiches*

Nowadays yeast bread is seldom made in the home and for this reason the method is not given here. There are, however, certain points about the use of bread which it is important for the housewife to know.

How to Keep the Loaf Fresh

Make sure the loaf is quite cold before putting it away. The best way to keep bread fresh is to wrap it in a clean, dry cloth and store in a well-ventilated place in a cupboard. Remember, bread must have air. If you keep it in a bin, be sure the bin is well ventilated; even with ventilation holes, keep the lid tilted. Keep the bin scrupulously clean. Wash it out once a week and dry it thoroughly.

To Avoid Dry Loaf Ends

When you get to the last three inches of your loaf, place it crumb side down on the bread board and cut this way. You'll eat the crust while it's fresh and you won't cut your fingers.

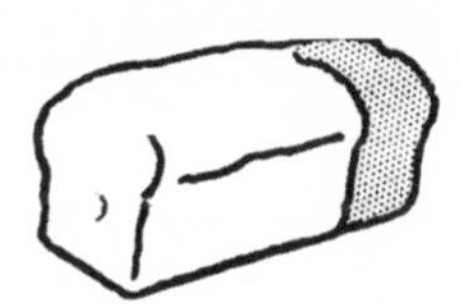
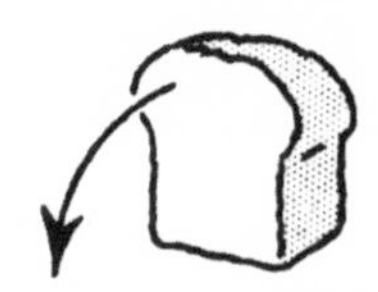
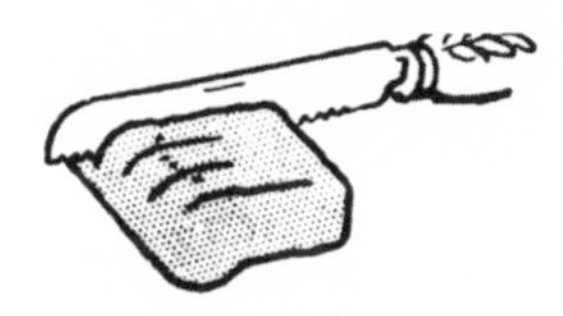

Preparation of Breadcrumbs

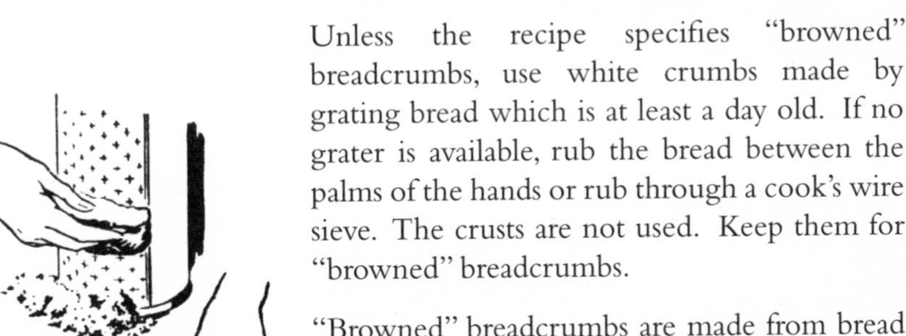

Unless the recipe specifies "browned" breadcrumbs, use white crumbs made by grating bread which is at least a day old. If no grater is available, rub the bread between the palms of the hands or rub through a cook's wire sieve. The crusts are not used. Keep them for "browned" breadcrumbs.

"Browned" breadcrumbs are made from bread slices or crusts which have been baked in a low oven until brown and crisp. Then put them through the mincer or crush with a rolling pin. Store in a covered tin or jar. These may be used for coating fish cakes, rissoles, croquettes, for covering the tops of au gratin dishes and similar savoury dishes and for sweet puddings. These crumbs are sometimes called "Raspings" (see page 14).

Making Toast

Bread at least a day old will toast more evenly than new bread. If toast is preferred soft, cut the bread in thick slices, ¼ in. to ½ in. thick, and toast very quickly near a fierce heat. If preferred crisp, cut the bread ¼ in. thick and dry the slices a little before toasting or turn them frequently during toasting. They will then dry as they toast.

Melba toast is made by drying thin slices of bread ⅛ in.–¼ in. thick, in a very slow oven until they are brown and crisp.

Uses for Stale Bread

The following are some ways of using up stale bread, and recipes will be found in most good cookery books: baked to make Melba toast and stored in an airtight tin. Cut in dice, baked crisp and used for a breakfast cereal. Used for savoury stuffings. The crust may be used as well if the bread is first soaked and then squeezed; and in many different kinds of sweet puddings and savoury dishes.

Tips on Making Sandwiches

1. Have bread a day old for easy cutting, or if available buy ready-sliced bread.
2. Warm the butter or margarine slightly and cream it well to make it spread easily.
3. For substantial sandwiches cut the bread ¼ in.–½ in. thick; for dainty sandwiches ⅛ in. thick.
4. Use a very sharp knife for quick, even slicing.
5. Do not trim off the crusts.
6. To keep sandwiches moist, wrap them in a damp cloth or in waxed paper. Wrap different kinds separately or the flavours will mix.
7. Use a generous amount of filling and if the sandwiches are for lunch or supper be sure they contain one of the following, in addition to a shredded raw green vegetable or chopped parsley: eggs, meat, fish, cheese, peas, beans or lentils.

19 *How to Plan Meals*

We have learnt in five years of war that it matters what you eat. People do not only need enough food to satisfy their hunger and make them feel well filled. They need enough of certain kinds of food to supply their bodies with vitality and to keep them well. The housewife to-day knows this. The word "vitamins" does not daunt her. She understands that the day's menu should be "balanced". When she goes out with her shopping basket, she goes on a planned expedition. The woman with the shopping basket has learnt a lot. We want to sum up for her in simple terms what she has learnt so that if there is any confusion in her mind she can read this chapter of her cookery book and be sure of giving her family the best food for health and vigour.

Foods for Fitness

Foods do three main things for the human body; firstly they provide it with fuel which burns to give energy and warmth; secondly they supply the various materials for building the growing body and replacing parts which are constantly being worn out; thirdly they supply substances called vitamins which enable the body to do the first two jobs properly and help to give fitness, vitality and resistance to disease. All foods give fuel for energy and heat although some are much better sources than others. Certain foods, however, give us very little body-building material or vitamins and are only useful for fuel purposes. Therefore, we must be sure that we are not living only on fuel foods, but that our meals contain enough building materials and vitamins for proper health. Because these latter substances are so important, the foods supplying them should always have first consideration.

Foods for Building and Repairing the Body

There are three main parts of the body that need materials for building and repairing. These are the bones and teeth, the muscles and the blood.

For bones and teeth we need the substance called "calcium", more commonly known as lime. This substance is very like the material that makes sea shells and marble. It makes bones and teeth hard, white and strong. We get it from milk, which nature designed to enable bones to grow, from cheese which is made from milk, and also a little from green vegetables. In order to use calcium properly, the body needs Vitamin D, the "sunshine vitamin".

For muscles, foods must contain a substance called "protein", which is found in large amounts in all animal foods except fats and in some vegetable foods. The protein found in animal foods such as milk of all kinds, cheese, meat, fish, eggs and dried eggs, is of very good quality. Dried peas, beans and lentils, bread and oatmeal also contain protein, but this is not quite such a good builder as that found in the animal foods. However, the body uses a mixture of the two kinds very well. So space your animal foods throughout the week eking them out with vegetable builders.

For building **good red blood**, iron is needed. The best foods for iron are liver, eggs, meat, green vegetables, national or wholemeal bread and oatmeal. Lack of iron makes people anaemic and tired, so don't let your family suffer from shortage of these foods.

The Vitamins

There are four vitamins especially which must be included regularly in the diet for health. These are Vitamin A, Vitamin B, Vitamin C and Vitamin D.

Vitamin A is needed for growth, for keeping the linings of the breathing, digestive and reproductive systems in good condition, and for the health of the eyes. It is found in cod liver oil, oily fish such as pilchards, herrings or salmon, dairy foods, and green and yellow vegetables. Liver, which is the animal's chief storehouse for important food material, is also rich in Vitamin A.

Vitamin B is needed for good digestion and steady nerves. It is got from National bread or flour, oatmeal, potatoes, peas, beans and lentils, yeast, eggs; vegetables also give a certain amount.

Vitamin C is needed for buoyant health, good skin, vitality and endurance. It comes chiefly from green vegetables, citrus fruit and potatoes. Orange juice concentrate, black-currant and rose-hip syrup are all very rich in Vitamin C. Babies should have these until they can take large quantities of vegetables.

Vitamin D is needed by children especially as it "anchors" the calcium in the proper places in growing bones and teeth and makes them strong. It comes from cod liver oil, butter and margarine, and fat fish such as pilchards, herrings, salmon, etc. Sunshine on a child's skin also helps to give this vitamin, but in this climate there is not very much sunshine, and so it is important that children, especially young ones, should have cod liver oil every day.

Foods for Energy and Warmth

When foods supplying all the body-building materials and vitamins have been included in the meal plan, then other foods should be added in quantities to meet the appetites of the various members of the family. If children are growing at the expected rate and adults are holding their weight at a reasonable level, then probably they are having enough total food. Heavy workers and adolescents need more than other people and it is a good idea that they should have regular mid-morning and mid-afternoon snacks. Fat is the food that supplies most energy and heat, and it is more satisfying than other foods. So have fat in some form at each meal to prevent you getting tired and hungry quickly.

In wartime, three rules for fitness have been given:
(1) Eat all your rations and priority foods.
(2) Salads and vegetables every day.
(3) Fill up with energy foods, bread, potatoes, oatmeal, etc.

If important foods from the war-time rations are made the foundation of our peacetime meals and if salads, vegetables and energy foods are added, the diet will be excellent. Therefore, we can still follow the three rules for fitness, and if, when rationing disappears, we remember these foods which we were accustomed to buy with our ration books and continue to purchase them, plus vegetables, salads and energy foods, we shall continue to have a good diet.

Pattern of Meals to Follow the Rules for Healthy Eating

Here is a suggestion for planning your meals to include all these body-building materials and vitamins every day. The dinner and supper meals can be reversed to suit individual households. For young children, tea should be the evening meal and supper, if any, would consist of a milky drink.

BREAKFAST MENU

PORRIDGE

(or other cereal or fruit with milk)

COOKED DISH

(Egg or bacon or fish, etc., with fried potatoes or fried bread)

NATIONAL or WHOLEMEAL BREAD

with

BUTTER or MARGARINE

and

MARMALADE or JAM

TEA or COFFEE

COCOA or MILK for children

MID-MORNING SNACK

Milk for children. Mid-meal snack for men or women doing heavy work. This should contain some building and vitamin foods, for example, cheese and salad sandwiches.

DINNER MENU

SOUP

(if desired)

MEAT

(or cheese or fish or egg)

FRESH VEGETABLES

(a green one several times weekly)

POTATOES

PUDDING

(Baked or steamed or cold pudding or fruit in season—with milk or custard)

In planning dinner, choose the animal food or "muscle builder" first, then choose a vegetable to go with it and potatoes. The pudding and soup are chosen to "fill up".

Note.—Dried peas, beans, lentils or oatmeal should be added to the meat, fish, cheese and egg dishes if the quantity of animal food is small through rationing or shortage.

TEA MENU

NATIONAL or WHOLEMEAL BREAD
with
BUTTER or MARGARINE
SPREAD or SANDWICH FILLING
(of shredded raw vegetables or yeast extract)
CAKES or BISCUITS or SCONES,
JAM (if desired)
TEA
MILK for children

SUPPER or LUNCH MENU

MAIN DISH
(of cheese or fish or egg or other muscle builders)
VEGETABLE or RAW SALAD
POTATOES
BREAD with BUTTER or MARGARINE
JAM or HONEY or SYRUP
TEA or COFFEE
MILK or COCOA for children

When the main course for dinner has been decided, the supper can then be selected to give variety, again starting with the "muscle-building" food. The choice of vegetable will depend on those served at dinner and tea. If a raw vegetable was used for tea-time sandwiches, a cooked one could be served at night. If another type of spread has been used, a raw salad should be included in the supper meal, even if this meal is hot. Salads go just as well with hot dishes as with cold when one becomes accustomed to the mixture.

Plenty of water should be drunk daily, between meals as well as at mealtime.

Orange juice for children and expectant mothers is usually taken first thing in the morning. They need cod liver oil (or Vitamin A and D tablets for the mothers) as well and these should be taken twice daily after meals. Babies should start these foods gradually.

RULES FOR GOOD MEAL PLANNING

1. PLAN AHEAD. If possible work out the meals for a week ahead or at least for one or two days. This is the only way to be sure that the right amounts of the right foods are used.

2. PLAN FOR ECONOMY. The less money there is to spend on food the more important good meal planning becomes. The temptation often is to buy

only the cheap foods, regardless of their food value and the body soon becomes badly nourished. Follow the meal patterns given on pages 91–92, but buy the cheapest foods out of each group, they are just as good.

For example, cheap cuts of meat are just as nourishing as the more expensive cuts. Learn to cook them economically (see pages 34–49). Herrings are the best value for money in fish. Ox liver is just as nourishing as the more expensive calves' liver. When fruit is dear, raw vegetable salads, cabbage and swede can be used to supply the same vitamin. Oatmeal is cheaper than prepared breakfast cereals. Cook it the quick way (page 72) and save on fuel.

Vitaminized margarine is cheaper than butter and often better food value. Take full advantage of free milk and school meal schemes available.

3. **PLAN TO SAVE LABOUR**. If one dish in the menu requires a great deal of preparation see that the others are quick and easy.

4. **PLAN MEALS WHICH LOOK GOOD**. Food which looks good usually tastes good and does you good.

Make full use of fresh green vegetables and brightly coloured foods like carrots and tomatoes for decorating dishes. Decoration, or garnishes as they are called, need not take a lot of time but a little chopped parsley or watercress to sprinkle on a colourless dish or a little raw grated carrot will work wonders.

5. **PLAN FOR VARIETY** and keep the family guessing. A monotonous diet is badly digested. If the foods you can use are limited learn new ways of serving them and make full use of flavourings (see page 19).

Introduce new dishes gradually, and serve them at the same meal as something which is already very popular.

PACKED MEALS

It is difficult to prepare a packed lunch which has all the foods needed for healthy eating and for this reason it is important to use available canteens and school meals.

If a packed meal must be taken see that it contains some of all the essential foods listed in the Pattern of Meals (pages 91–92). Jam sandwiches and tea are *not* an adequate substitute for the Lunch Menu on page 92.

PREPARING MEALS

When preparing meals many beginners find it difficult to have all the food ready at the same time. Few foods are improved by being kept hot and it is most important to organize the preparation so as to have each cooked at the right time. The following points should help, although practice is needed more than anything else:

1. Decide what you are going to cook for the meal before you start anything (see "Meal Planning", page 92).
2. Note how long each dish takes to cook and if you are new to the job it is a good plan to jot down the times when you should start the cooking to have each dish finished by 12 or 1 or whenever the meal is to be served. It is not always possible to know the exact time a dish will take but if you are in doubt start it in plenty of time.
3. If all the dishes take about the same time to cook be sure to do any preparation of ingredients before you start cooking; otherwise you will find one dish is late because it took 15 or 20 minutes to prepare the ingredients.
4. Try and wash up cooking utensils as you go along, because it is much easier to dish up quickly if your sink and table are free.
5. If you have a good warming cupboard or if the oven has been on, dish up the pudding before you sit down to the meal.
6. The easiest kind of meal is the all in one casserole or hot pot, where meat, vegetables and potatoes are cooked together. This can be excellent if cooked slowly and well flavoured.

Conversion Tables

Oven Temperatures

Gas mark	*° F.*	*° C.*
1	275° F.	140° C.
2	300° F.	150° C.
3	325° F.	170° C.
4	350° F.	180° C.
5	375° F.	190° C.
6	400° F.	200° C.
7	425° F.	220° C.
8	450° F.	230° C.
9	475° F.	240° C.

Weights

Imperial	*Metric*
½ oz.	10 g.
¾ oz.	20 g.
1 oz.	25 g.
1½ oz.	40 g.
2 oz.	50 g.
2½ oz.	60 g.
3 oz.	75 g.
4 oz. (¼ lb.)	110 g.
4½ oz.	125 g.
5 oz.	150 g.
6 oz.	175 g.
7 oz.	200 g.
8 oz. (½ lb.)	225 g.
9 oz.	250 g.
10 oz.	275 g.
12 oz. (¾ lb.)	350 g.
1 lb.	450 g.
2 lb.	900 g.
3 lb.	1.35 kg.

Liquid Conversions

Imperial	*Metric*
1 teaspoon	5 ml.
1 tablespoon	15 ml.
4 tablespoons	55 ml.
¼ pint	150 ml.
½ pint	275 ml.
¾ pint	450 ml.
1 pint	570 ml.
2 pints	1.2 litres
8 pints	4.8 litres

Dimensions

Imperial	*Metric*
⅛ inch	3 mm.
¼ inch	5 mm.
½ inch	1 cm.
¾ inch	2 cm.
1 inch	2.5 cm.
1¼ inch	3 cm.
1½ inch	4 cm.
1¾ inch	4.5 cm.
2 inch	5 cm.
2½ inch	6 cm.
3 inch	7.5 cm.
3½ inch	9 cm.
4 inch	10 cm.
5 inch	13 cm.
5¼ inch	13.5 cm.
6 inch	15 cm.
6½ inch	16 cm.
7 inch	18 cm.
7½ inch	19 cm.
8 inch	20 cm.
9 inch	23 cm.
9½ inch	24 cm.
10 inch	25.5 cm.
11 inch	28 cm.
12 inch	30 cm.

IMPERIAL WAR
MUSEUM